D0992580

ESSAYS
IN
SATIRE

ESSAYS IN SATIRE

BY

RONALD A. KNOX

KENNIKAT PRESS, INC./PORT WASHINGTON, N. Y.

ESSAYS IN SATIRE

First published 1928
Reissued 1968 by Kennikat Press

Library of Congress Catalog Card No: 68-26297
Manufactured in the United States of America

Dedicated to

L. E. EYRES

πολλῶν οὕνεκα

PREFACE

THIS BOOK is, I am afraid, a patchwork—in
date, in style, in treatment, in inspiration. I
cannot even claim that it only contains satire;
one of the items, at least, is no satire, though it
contains material for the making of satire; and
another, which was only meant to be a mild
farmyard imitation, became a satire on human
credulity only through its reception by the public.
In fact, there is only one common thread that
runs through the book. It is a practical answer
to the question, frequently asked, *Where can I
get hold of that thing you wrote some years ago
about Such and Such?* Well, here it is; but if
you want to buy it you must buy all the others
as well, for I will see to it that the printer binds
them all up in one volume. You cannot go
into a stationer's and ask for an Ace of Spades;
they will tell you to buy a whole pack, because
they do not keep spare parts. So here; if you
want to possess "The Mind and Art of Sherlock
Holmes" for instance, you must buy all the

others as well, and throw them away if you do not want them.

But what a collection it is, and how it dates its author! That Sherlock Holmes paper was written, I believe, in 1911, for the Gryphon Club at Trinity; it has been read to various societies, I suppose, above a score of times, and twice published, in *The Blue Book* and *Blackfriars*. *The Identity of the Pseudo-Bunyan* was published in *G. K.'s Weekly*; so was *The Authorship of "In Memoriam"*; but this was republished later in the *Oxford Magazine*. Two more appeared in *Blackfriars*, *A New Cure for Religion* and *The New Sin*. *A Ramble in Barsetshire* appeared in the *London Mercury*, and *Jottings from a Psycho-Analyst's Note-book* in the *Illustrated Review*. *Reunion All Round* was, from the first, published as a separate tract; *Absolute and Abitofhell* came out first in the *Oxford Magazine*, then in a collection of Oxford poetry, then as a tract. *Materials for a Boswellian Problem* will be published somewhere or other, if I can manage it, before this book gets printed.

CONTENTS

INTRODUCTION

INTRODUCTION

ON HUMOUR
AND SATIRE

WHOEVER SHALL turn up in a modern
encyclopædia the article on humming-
birds—whether from a disinterested curiosity
about these brightly-coloured creatures, or from
the more commonplace motive of identifying a
clue in a crossword—will find a curious surprise awaiting him at the end of it. He will
find that the succeeding paragraph deals with
the geological formation known as a *humus;* or if
his encyclopædia be somewhat more exhaustive,
with the quaintly-named genius of Humper-
dinck. What will excite his speculation is, of
course, the fact that no attempt is made by his
author to deal with humour. Humour, for the
encyclopædist, is non-existent; and that means
that no book has ever been written on the subject
of humour; else the ingenious Caledonian who
retails culture to us at the rate of five guineas
a column would inevitably have boiled it down
for us ere this. The great history of Humour
in three volumes, dedicated by permission to

the Bishop of Much Wenlock, still remains to be written. And that fact, in its turn, is doubly significant. It means, in the first place, that humour, in our sense of the word, is a relatively modern phenomenon; the idea of submitting it to exhaustive analysis did not, for example, present itself to the patient genius of John Stuart Mill. And at the same time it is an uncommonly awkward and elusive subject to tackle, or why have we no up-to-date guide to it from the hand of Mr. Arnold Bennett?

Assuredly this neglect is not due to any want of intrinsic importance. For humour, frown upon it as you will, is nothing less than a fresh window of the soul. Through that window we see, not indeed a different world, but the familiar world of our experience distorted as if by the magic of some tricksy sprite. It is a plate-glass window, which turns all our earnest, toiling fellow-mortals into figures of fun. If a man awoke to it of a sudden, it would be an enlightenment of his vision no less real than if a man who had hitherto seen life only in black and grey should be suddenly gifted with the experience of colour. More, even, than this; the sense of humour is a man's inseparable playmate, allowing him, for better or worse, no solitude anywhere. In crowded railway-carriages, in the lonely watches of a sleepless night, even in the dentist's chair, the sense of humour is at your side, full of elfin suggestions. Do you go to Church? He will patter up the aisle alongside of you, never more at home, never more alert, than when the spacious silences of worship and the solemn purple of prelates enjoins reverence. I could become lyrical, if I had time, over the sense of humour, what it does for men and how it undoes them, what comfort lies in its companionship, and what menace. Enough to say that if I had the writing of an encyclopædia the humming-birds should be made to look foolish.

Humour has been treated, perhaps, twice in literature; once in the preface to Meredith's *Egoist*, and once in Mr. Chesterton's book, *The Napoleon of Notting Hill*. What it is still remains a mystery. Easy enough to distinguish it from its neighbours in the scale of values: with wit, for example, it has nothing to do. For wit is first and last a matter of expression. Latin, of all languages, is the best vehicle of wit, the worst of humour. You cannot think a witty thought, even, without thinking in words. But humour can be wordless; there

are thoughts that lie too deep for laughter itself.
In this essay I mean to treat humour as it compares with and contrasts with satire, a more
delicate distinction. But first let us make an
attempt, Aristotle-wise, to pin down the thing
itself with some random stab of definition. Let
us say that the sphere of humour is, predom-
inantly, Man and his activities, considered in
circumstances so incongruous, so unexpectedly
incongruous, as to detract from their human
dignity. Thus, the prime source of humour is
a madman or a drunkard; either of these wears
the semblance of a man without enjoying the
full use of that rational faculty which is man's
definition. A foreigner, too, is always funny:
he dresses, but does not dress right; makes
sounds, but not the right sounds. A man falling
down on a frosty day is funny, because he has
unexpectedly abandoned that upright walk
which is man's glory as a biped. All these
things are funny, of course, only from a certain
angle; not, for example, from the angle of ninety
degrees, which is described by the man who falls
down. But amusement is habitually derived
from such situations; and in each case it is a
human victim that is demanded for the sacrifice. It is possible, in the mythological manner,

to substitute an animal victim, but only if the animal be falsely invested with the attributes of humanity. There is nothing at all funny about a horse falling down. A monkey making faces, a cat at play, amuse us only because we feign to ourselves that the brute is rational; to that fiction we are accustomed from childhood. Only Man has dignity; only man, therefore, can be funny. Whether there could have been humour even in human fortunes but for the Fall of Adam is a problem which might profitably have been discussed by St. Thomas in his *Summa Theologiae*, but was omitted for lack of space.

The question is raised (as the same author would say) whether humour is in its origins indecent. And at first sight it would appear yes. For the philosopher says that the ludicrous is a division of the disgraceful. And the gods in Homer laugh at the predicament of Ares and Aphrodite in the recital of the bard Demodocus. But on second thoughts it is to be reflected that the song of Demodocus is, by common consent of the critics, a late interpolation in Homer; and the first mention of laughter in the classics is rather the occasion on which the gods laughed to see the lame Hephaestus panting as he limped

up and down the hall. Once more, a lame man
is funny because he enjoys, like the rest of us,
powers of locomotion, but employs them wrong.
His gait is incongruous—not unexpectedly so,
indeed, for the gods had witnessed this farce
daily for centuries ; but the gods were children,
and the simplest farces always have the best
run. No doubt the psycho-analysts will want
us to believe that all humour has its origin in
indecency, and, for aught I know, that when-
ever we laugh we are unconsciously thinking of
something obscene. But, in fact, the obscene,
as its name implies, is an illegitimate effect of
humour. There is nothing incongruous in the
existence of sex and the other animal functions ;
the incongruity lies merely in the fact of men-
tioning them. It is not human dignity that is
infringed in such cases, but a human convention
of secrecy. The Stock Exchange joke, like most
operations on the Stock Exchange, is essentially
artificial ; it does not touch the real values of
things at all. In all the generalizations which
follow it must be understood that the humour
of indecency is being left out of account.

Yet there is truth in the philosopher's asser-
tion that the ludicrous is a division of the disgraceful, in this sense, that in the long run

every joke makes a fool of somebody; it must
have, as I say, a human victim. This fact is
obscured by the frequency with which jokes,
especially modern jokes, are directed against
their own authors. The man who makes faces to
amuse a child is, objectively, making a fool of
himself; and that whole *genre* of literary humour
of which *Happy Thoughts*, the *Diary of a Nobody*,
and the Eliza books are the best-known examples,
depends entirely on the fact that the author is
making a fool of himself. In all humour there
is loss of dignity somewhere, virtue has gone
out of somebody. For there is no inherent
humour in things; wherever there is a joke it is
Man, the half-angel, the half-beast, who is somehow at the bottom of it. I am insisting upon this
point because, on a careless analysis, one might
be disposed to imagine that the essence of
satire is to be a joke directed against somebody.
That definition, clearly, will be inadequate, if our
present analysis of humour in general be
accepted.

I have said that humour is, for the most part,
a modern phenomenon. It would involve a
very long argument, and some very far-reaching
considerations, if we attempted to prove this
thesis of humour as a fact in life. Let us be

more modest, and be content for the present to
say that the humorous in literature is for the
most part a modern phenomenon. Let us go
back to our starting-point, and imagine one
pursuing his researches about humming-birds
into the *Encyclopædia Britannica* of 1797. He
skims through a long article on Mr. David
Hume, faced by an attractive but wholly
unreliable portrait of the hippopotamus. Under
" Humming-bird " he will only read the words
" See Trochilus." But immediately following,
he will find the greater part of a column under
the title " Humour." Most of it deals with the
jargon of a psychology now obsolete, and perhaps fanciful, though not more fanciful, I
think, than the psychological jargon of our own
day. But at the end he will find some valuable
words on humour as it is contrasted with wit.
" Wit expresses something that is more designed,
concerted, regular, and artificial; humour,
something that is more wild, loose, extravagant,
and fantastical; something which comes upon
a man by fits, which he can neither command
nor restrain, and which is not perfectly consistent with true politeness. Humour, it has
been said, is often more diverting than wit;
yet a man of wit is as much above a man of

humour, as a gentleman is above a buffoon ; a
buffoon, however, will often divert more than
a gentleman. The Duke of Buckingham, however, makes humour to be all in all," and so on.
" Not perfectly consistent with true politeness "
—oh, admirable faith of the eighteenth century,
even in its decline ! " The Duke of Buckingham,
however"—a significant exception. It seems
possible that the reign of the Merry Monarch
saw a false dawn of the sense of humour. If
so, it was smothered for a full century after-
wards by an overpowering incubus of whiggery.
The French Revolution had come and gone, and
yet humour was for the age of Burke " not
perfectly consistent with true politeness."

One is tempted, as I say, to maintain that
the passing of the eighteenth century is an era
in human history altogether, since with the
nineteenth century humour, as an attitude
towards life, begins. The tone of Disraeli about
politics, the tone of Richard Hurrell Froude
about all the external part of religion, seems
to me quite inconceivable in any earlier age.
But let us confine ourselves to literature, and
say that humour as a force *in literature* is struggling
towards its birth in Jane Austen, and hardly
achieves its full stature till Calverley. I know

that there are obvious exceptions. There is
humour in Aristophanes and in Petronius;
there is humour in Shakespeare, though not as
much of it as one would expect; humour in
Sterne, too, and in Sheridan. But if you set
out to mention the great names of antiquity
which are naturally connected with humorous
writing, you will find that they are all the names
of satirists. Aristophanes in great part, Lucian,
Juvenal, Martial, Blessed Thomas More, Cer-
vantes, Rabelais, Butler, Molière, La Fontaine,
Swift—humour and satire are, before the nineteenth century, almost interchangeable terms.
Humour in art had begun in the eighteenth
century, but it had begun with Hogarth! Put
a volume by Barrie or Milne into the hands of
Edmund Burke—could he have begun to understand it?

You can corroborate the fact of this growth in
humour by a complementary fact about our
modern age, the decline of *naïveté*. If you come
to think of it, the best laughs you will get out
of the old classics are laughs which the author
never meant to put there. Of all the ancients,
none can be so amusing as Herodotus, but none,
surely, had less sense of humour. It is a rare
grace, like all the *gratiae gratis datae*, this humour

of the *naïf*. Yet it reaches its climax on the very
threshold of the nineteenth century; next to
Herodotus, surely, comes James Boswell.   Since
the dawn of nineteenth century humour, you
will find unconscious humour only in bad
writers, Ella Wheeler Wilcox, and the rest.
Humour kills the *naïf*, nor could any great
writer of to-day recapture, if he would, Boswell's
splendid unselfconsciousness.

Under correction, then, I am maintaining
that literature before the nineteenth century
has no conscious humour apart from satire.   I
must now pass on to an impression which all of
us have, but an impression so presumptuous that
we seldom have the courage to put it into words.
It is this, that humour, apart from satire, belongs
to the English-speaking peoples alone.   I say,
the English-speaking peoples, a cumbrous and
an unreal division of mankind.   But, thank
God, you cannot bring any preposterous ethno-
graphical fictions in here.   Not even Houston
Stewart Chamberlain ever ventured to congratulate the Germans on their sense of humour;
not even the Dean of St. Paul's will dare to tell
us that the sense of humour is Nordic.   The facts
speak for themselves.   Satire still flourishes on
the Continent; Anatole France was no un-

worthy citizen of the country of Voltaire. There is satire, too, among the Northern peoples; I believe that if I expressed my private opinion as to who was the world's greatest satirist I should reply, Hans Andersen. Only in spots, of course; but the man who wrote the *Ugly Duckling* and the *Darning Needle* and the *Story of the Emperor's New Clothes* seems to me to have a finer sense of the intrinsic ludicrousness of mankind than Swift himself. Satire is international, as it is of all ages; but where shall humour be found, apart from satire, on the Continent of Europe? Who, unless he were a laugher at the malicious or the obscene, ever picked up the translation of a foreign book in search of a good laugh? Who ever found a good joke in a Continental illustrated paper? Cleverness of drawing abounds, but the captions beneath the drawings are infantile. I have seen a Swedish illustrated supplement, and I do not believe there was a single item in it which would have been accepted by *Comic Cuts*. I am told that the humorous drama of modern France forms a complete exception to this statement of the facts. I am content to believe it; there must, of course, be exceptions. I put forward the rule as a rule.

Some, no doubt, on a hasty analysis, would limit the field still further by saying that humour is purely English. And it would be easy to defend this contention by pointing to the fact that the English enjoy their joke very largely at the expense of their neighbours. Nothing belongs more decisively to the English-speaking world than the anecdote. We are for ever telling stories, and how many of those stories are about a Scot (we call it a Scotchman), an Irishman, a Jew, or an American? But this, if our definition of humour was a sound one, is in the nature of the case. A foreigner is funny, because he is like ourselves only different. A Scot or an Irishman is funny to the Englishman because he is almost exactly like himself, only slightly different. He talks English as his native tongue, only with an incorrect accent; what could possibly be funnier? A Scot is more funny than a Frenchman just as a monkey is more amusing than a dog; he is nearer the real thing.

But, in fact, all such judgments have been distorted beyond recognition by national hypocrisy. It is the English tradition that the Irish are a nation brimming over with humour, quite incapable of taking anything seriously. Irish people are in the habit of saying things which English people think funny. Irish people do not think them funny in the least. It follows, from the English point of view, that Ireland is a nation of incorrigible humorists, all quite incapable of governing themselves. The Scot, on the other hand, has an unfortunate habit of governing the English, and the English, out of revenge, have invented the theory that the Scot has no sense of humour. The Scot cannot have any sense of humour, because he is very careful about money, and drinks whisky where ordinary people drink beer. All the stories told against the Scottish nation are, I am told, invented in Aberdeen, and I partly believe it. There is (if a denationalized Ulsterman like myself may make the criticism) a pawkiness about all the stories against Scotland which betrays their Caledonian origin. The fact is that the Scottish sense of humour differs slightly from the English sense of humour, but I am afraid I have no time to indicate the difference. There is humour in the country of Stevenson and Barrie; and if the joke is often against Scotland, what better proof could there be that it is humour, and not satire?

Whatever may be said of Americans in real life, it is certain that their literature has humour.

Personally I do not think that the Americans are
nearly as proud as they ought to be of this fact ;
Mark Twain ought to be to the American what
Burns is to the Scot, and rather more.   The
hall-mark of American humour is its pose of
illiteracy.   All the American humorists spend
their time making jokes against themselves.
Artemus Ward pretended that he was unable
even to spell.   Mark Twain pretended that he
had received no education beyond spelling, and
most of his best remarks are based on this
affectation of ignorance.   " What is your *bête
noire?* " asked the revelations-of-character book,
and Mark Twain replied, " What is my which? "
" He spelt it Vinci, but pronounced it Vinchy ;
foreigners always spell better than they pro-
nounce "—that is perhaps one of the greatest
jokes of literature, but the whole point of it lies
in a man pretending to be worse educated than
he really is.   Mr. Leacock, as a rule, amuses by
laughing at himself.   America, on the other
hand, has very little to show in the way of
satire.   Lowell was satirical, in a rather heavy
vein, and Mr. Leacock is satirical occasionally,
in a way that seems to me purely English.   I
want to allude to that later on ; for the present
let it be enough to note that the Americans,

like the English and the Scots, do possess a literary tradition of non-satirical humour.

Thus far, we have concluded that the humorous in literature is the preserve of that period which succeeds the French Revolution, and of those peoples which speak the English language under its several denominations; unless by the word humour you understand "satire." It is high time, obviously, that we attempted some definition of what satire is, or at least of the marks by which it can be distinguished from non-satirical humour. It is clear from the outset that the author who laughs at himself, unless the self is a deliberately assumed one, is not writing satire. *Happy Thoughts* and *The Diary of a Nobody* may be what you will; they are not satire. *The Tramp Abroad* is not satire; *My Lady Nicotine* is not satire. For in all these instances the author, with a charity worthy of the Saints—and indeed, St. Philip Neri's life is full of this kind of charity—makes a present of himself to his reader as a laughing-stock. In satire, on the contrary, the writer always leaves it to be assumed that he himself is immune from all the follies and the foibles which he pillories. To take an obvious instance, Dickens is no satirist when he introduces you to

Mr. Winkle, because there is not the smallest reason to suppose that Dickens would have handled a gun better than Mr. Winkle. But when Dickens introduces you to Mr. Bumble he is a satirist at once, for it is perfectly obvious that Dickens would have handled a porridge-ladle better than Mr. Bumble did. The humorist runs with the hare; the satirist hunts with the hounds.

There is, indeed, less contempt in satire than in irony. Irony is content to describe men exactly as they are, to accept them professedly, at their own valuation, and then to laugh up its sleeve. It falls outside the limits of humorous literature altogether; there is irony in Plato, there is irony in the Gospels; Mr. Galsworthy is an ironist, but few people have ever laughed over Mr. Galsworthy. Satire, on the contrary, borrows its weapons from the humorist; the satirized figure must be made to leap through the hoops of improbable adventure and farcical situation. It is all the difference between *The Egoist* and *Don Quixote*. Yet the laughter which satire provokes has malice in it always; we want to dissociate ourselves from the victim; to let the lash that curls round him leave our withers unwrung. It is not so with humour:

not so (for instance) with the work of an author
who should have been mentioned earlier, Mr.
P. G. Wodehouse. To read the adventures of
Bertie Wooster as if they were a satire on Bertie
Wooster, or even on the class to which Bertie
Wooster may be supposed to belong, is to mis-
read them in a degree hardly possible to a
German critic. The reader must make himself
into Bertie Wooster in order to enjoy his Jeeves,
just as he must make himself into Eliza's husband
in order to enjoy his Eliza. Nobody can appreciate the crackers of humour unless he is content
to put on his fool's cap with the rest of the
party.

What, then, is the relation between humour
and satire? Which is the parent, and which the
child? Which is the normal organ, and which
the morbid growth? I said just now that satire
borrows its weapons from the humorist, and
that is certainly the account most of us would
be prepared to give of the matter off-hand.
Most things in life, we reflect, have their comic
side as well as their serious side; and the good-
humoured man is he who is content to see the
humorous side of things even when the joke
is against himself. The comic author, by per-
sistently abstracting from the serious side of

things, contrives to build up a world of his own,
whose figures are all grotesques, whose adventures are the happy adventures of farce.   Men
fight, but only with foils; men suffer, but only
suffer indignities; it is all a pleasant nursery
tale, a relief to be able to turn to it when your
mind is jaded with the sour facts of real life.
Such, we fancy, is the true province of the Comic
Muse; and satire is an abuse of the function.
The satirist is like one who should steal his little
boy's water-pistol and load it with vitriol, and
so walk abroad flourishing it in men's faces.
A treacherous fellow, your satirist.   He will
beguile the leisure of an Athenian audience,
needing some rest, Heaven knows, from the
myriad problems of a relentless war with powerful neighbours, by putting on a little play called
The Birds.   Capital; we shall enjoy that.   Two
citizens of Athens, so the plot runs, take wings
to themselves and set out to build a bird city,
remote from the daily instance of this subnubilar
world.   Excellent! That is just what we wanted,
a relief for tired brains!   And then, the fellow
has tricked us, it proves, after all!   His city in
the clouds is, after all, only a parody of an
Athenian colony, and the ceremonies which
attend its inauguration are a burlesque, in the

worst possible taste, of Athenian colonial policy.
We came here for a holiday, and we are being
treated to a sermon instead! No wonder the
Athenian audiences often refused the first prize
to Aristophanes. Skip twenty-one centuries, and
find yourself in the times of the early Georges.
There has been a great vogue, of late, for des-
criptions of travel in strange countries; and
now (they are saying in the coffee-houses) the
Dean of St. Patrick's, Dublin, has written a
burlesque of these travel narratives, about
countries that never existed at all—the ingenious
dog! And then, as we read, it dawns upon us
suddenly that Lilliput and Brobdingnag are not,
after all, so distant, so imaginary; in fact, we
have never really got away from the England oı
the Georges at all. The spirit of satire has over-
looked us, like a wicked fairy, and turned the
milk of human kindness sour as we churned it.

My present thesis, not dogmatically asserted
but rather thrown out as if for discussion, is
that this way of viewing the relations between
humour and satire is a perversion of history.
To think of satire as a particular direction
which humour may happen to take, a particular
channel into which humour may be diverted, is
to neglect, surely, the broad facts as we have

stated them above. Humour is of an age, satire
of all ages; humour is of one particular civilization, satire of all countries. Is it not, then, more
reasonable to suppose that satire is a normal
function of the human genius, and humour that
has no satire in it a perversion of the function,
a growth away from the normal? That our
sense of the ridiculous is not, in its original
application, a child's toy at all, but a weapon,
deadly in its efficacy, entrusted to us for exposing
the shams and hypocrisies of the world? The
tyrant may arm himself in triple mail, may sur-
round himself with bodyguards, may sow his
kingdom with a hedge of spies, so that free speech
is crushed and criticism muzzled. Nay, worse,
he may so debauch the consciences of his subjects
with false history and with sophistical argument
that they come to believe him the thing he gives
himself out for, a creature half-divine, a heaven-
sent deliverer. One thing there is that he still
fears; one anxiety still bids him turn this way
and that to scan the faces of his slaves. He is
afraid of laughter. The satirist stands there,
like the little child in the procession when the
Emperor walked through the capital in his
famous new clothes; his is the tiny voice that
interprets the consciousness of a thousand

onlookers : " But, Mother, he has no clothes
on at all ! "

Satire has a wider scope, too. It is born to
scourge the persistent and ever-recurrent follies
of the human creature as such. And, for anybody who has the humility to realize that it is
aimed at him, and not merely at his neighbours,
satire has an intensely remedial effect; it purifies
the spiritual system of man as nothing else that is
human can possibly do. Thus, every young
man who is in love should certainly read *The
Egoist* (there would be far less unhappiness in
marriage if they all did), and no schoolmaster
should ever begin the scholastic year without
re-reading Mr. Bradby's *Lanchester Tradition*, to
remind him that he is but dust. Satire is thus an
excellent discipline for the satirized : whether
it is a good thing for the satirist is more open
to question. *Facit indignatio versum;* it is seldom
that the impetus to write satire comes to a man
except as the result of a disappointment. Since
disappointment so often springs from love, it is
not to be wondered at that satirists have ever
dealt unkindly with woman, from the days of
Simonides of Amorgos, who compared woman
with more than thirty different kinds of animals,
in every case to her disadvantage. A pinched,

warped fellow, as a rule, your satirist. It is misery that drives men to laughter. It is bad humour that encourages men first to be humorous. And it is, I think, when good-humoured men pick up this weapon of laughter, and, having no vendettas to work off with it, begin tossing it idly at a mark, that humour without satire takes its origin.

In a word, humour without satire is, strictly speaking, a perversion, the misuse of a sense. Laughter is a deadly explosive which was meant to be wrapped up in the cartridge of satire, and so, aimed unerringly at its appointed target, deal its salutary wound; humour without satire is a flash in the pan; it may be pretty to look at, but it is, in truth, a waste of ammunition. Or, if you will, humour is satire that has run to seed; trained no longer by an artificial process, it has lost the virility of its stock. It is port from the wood, without the depth and mystery of its vintage rivals. It is a burning-glass that has lost its focus; a passenger, pulling no weight in the up-stream journey of life; meat that has had the vitamins boiled out of it; a clock without hands. The humorist, in short, is a satirist out of a job; he does not fit into the scheme of things; the world passes him by.

The pure humorist is a man without a message. He can preach no gospel, unless it be the gospel that nothing matters; and that in itself is a foolish theme, for if nothing matters, what does it matter whether it matters or not? Mr. Wodehouse is an instance in point, Mr. Leacock nearly so, though there is a story in *Arcadian Adventures with the Idle Rich* about the amalgamation of two religious bodies on strictly commercial lines, which comes very close to pure satire. Barry Pain is a humorist who is seldom at his best when he attempts satire; the same fate dogged Mark Twain, though I think he would have liked to be a satirist. Mr. A. A. Milne is in a similar case, and so indeed are all the modern *Punch* writers by the terms (you might say) of their contract. No contrast is more surprising than the contrast in atmosphere between the letterpress of *Punch* before 1890 and its letterpress since. The old *Punches* are full of very bad satire; there is hardly anything else in them; it is all on the same sort of level as *John Bull* in its Bottomley days—anti-aristocratic, anti-foreign, anti-clerical, very much like some rag of the Boulevards. To-day, it is the home of superbly finished humour—humour cultivated as a fine art. But satire is absent.

Some of the greatest humorists have halted between two destinies, and as a rule have been lost to satire. Sir W. S. Gilbert, a rather unsuccessful satirist in his early days, inherited the dilemma from his master, Aristophanes. *Patience* is supreme satire, and there is satire in all the operas; but in their general effect they do not tell: the author has given up to mankind what was meant for a party. Mr. Chesterton is in the same difficulty; he is like Johnson's friend who tried to be a philosopher, but cheerfulness would keep on coming in. The net effect of his works is serious, as it is meant to be, but his fairy-like imagination is for ever defeating its own object in matters of detail. But indeed, Mr. Chesterton is beyond our present scope; for he is rash enough to combine humour not merely with satire but with serious writing; and that, it is well known, is a thing the public will not stand. A few modern authors have succeeded, in spite of our latter-day demand for pure humour, in being satirists first and last: Samuel Butler of *Erewhon*, and W. H. Mallock, and Mr. Belloc, I think, in his political novels. The very poor reception given to these last by the public proves that there is more vinegar in them than oil.

Humour, if we may adopt for a moment the loathsome phraseology of journalism, has " come to stay." It is, if our analysis be true, a by-product and in a sense a waste-product; that does not mean that it has no significance. A pearl is a by-product, and from the fishmonger's point of view a waste-product; but it has value so long as people want it. And there is at present a public demand for humour which implies that humour should take its place among the arts, an art for the art's sake, not depending on any fruits of practical utility for its estimation. There is art in O. Henry, though he does not scourge our vices like Juvenal; there is art in Heath Robinson, though he does not purge our consciences like Hogarth. What rank humour is to take as compared with serious writing is, perhaps, an unanswerable problem; our histories of nineteenth century literature have not yet been bold enough to tackle it. It is probable, I think, that humour is relatively ephemeral; by force of words humour means caprice, and the caprice of yesterday is apt to leave us cold. There is a generation not yet quite dead which says that nothing was ever so funny as the *Bongaultier Ballads*. The popularity of the *Ingoldsby Legends* is now, to say the least, pre-

carious; and I doubt if the modern youth
smacks its lips as we did over the *Bab Ballads*
themselves. Read a book of A. A. Milne's, and
then turn to an old volume of *Voces Populi*, and
you will realize that even in our memory humour
has progressed and become rarefied. What
reputations will be left unassailable when the
tide has receded, it would be rash to prophesy.
For myself, I like to believe that one name will
be immortal at least, that of Mr. Max Beer-
bohm. Incomparably equipped for satire, as
his cartoons and his parodies show, he has yet
preferred in most of his work to give rein to a
gloriously fantastic imagination, a humorist in
satirist's clothing. One is tempted to say
with the prophet: May I die the death of the
righteous, and may my last end be like his!

Meanwhile, a pertinent question may be
raised, What will be the effect of all this modern
vogue for pure humour upon the prospects of
satiric writing? We are in danger, it seems to
me, of debauching our sense of the ridiculous
to such an extent as to leave no room for the
disciplinary effect of satire. I remember seeing
Mr. Shaw's *Press Cuttings* first produced in Manchester. I remember a remark, in answer to the
objection that women ought not to vote because

they do not fight, that a woman risks her life
every time a man is born, being received (in
Manchester!) with shouts of happy laughter.
In that laughter I read the tragedy of Mr.
Bernard Shaw. He lashes us with virulent
abuse, and we find it exquisitely amusing.
Other ages have stoned the prophets; ours pelts
them instead with the cauliflower bouquets of
the heavy comedian. No country, I suppose,
has greater need of a satirist to-day than the
United States of America; no country has a
greater output of humour, good and bad, which
is wholly devoid of any satirical quality. If a
great American satirist should arise, would his
voice be heard among the hearty guffaws which
are dismally and eternally provoked by Mutt,
Jeff, Felix, and other kindred abominations?
And have we, on this side of the Atlantic, any
organ in which pure satire could find a natural
home? I believe the danger which I am indi-
cating to be a perfectly real one, however fantastic it may sound—the danger, I mean, that
we have lost, or are losing, the power to take
ridicule seriously. That our habituation to
humorous reading has inoculated our systems
against the beneficent poison of satire. Unhappy the Juvenal whom Rome greets with

amusement; unhappier still the Rome, that can be amused by a Juvenal!

I am not sure, in reading through this essay again, that there is any truth in its suggestions. But I do not see that there can be any harm in having said what I thought, even if I am no longer certain that I think it.

I

REUNION ALL ROUND

Being a Plea for the Inclufion within
the *Church of England* of all *Mahometans,
Jews, Buddhifts, Brahmins, Papifts* and
Atheifts, fubmitted to the confideration
of the British Public

I

REUNION ALL ROUND

IT is now generally conceded, that thofe Differences, which were once held to divide the Chriftian Sects from one another, (as, Whether or no *Confirmation* were a neceffary Ordinance of the Church) can no longer be thought to place any Obftacle againft Unity and Charity between Chriftians; rather, the more of 'em we find to exift, the more laudable a thing it is that Chriftian men should ftomach, now and again, thefe uneafy Scruples, and worship together for all the World as if they had never exifted. There is no Progrefs in Humanity, without the furmounting of Obftacles; thus, we are all now agree'd that *Satan*, far from meaning any harm to our Race when he brought Sin into the World, was moft excellently difpof'd towards us, and defir'd nothing better than that we, having fome good ftout Sins to overcome, should attain an eventful

47

and exciting fort of Virtue, inftead of languish-
ing for ever in that ftate of refpectable Innocence, which is fo little creditable to the Angels,
who alone practife it. In like manner, all
Herefies and *Schifms* are the very Condition of
Chriftian Unity, and were doubtlefs defigned
to fupply a kind of Zeft to the tedious bufinefs
of Church-going, on the fame Principle that
the Digeftion of *Poultry* is improv'd, if they be
allow'd to have a little Grit or Gravel in their
Crops to affift them. So that there can be
no more edifying Spectacle, to the rightly-
conftituted mind, than that of two Fellow-wor-
shippers, one of whom is faying in his heart,
Great is *Diana* of the *Ephefians*, and the other,
O *Baal*, hear us, both which inward Intentions
they exprefs by a common Formula, when
they profefs openly with their lips, *That Honefty
is the beft Policy.*

Further, it has come to be feen that *Bishops*
and *Archbishops* are not, as was commonly fuppof'd hitherto, the Vehicles of any extraordinary
Grace, which they paff'd on one to another,
like a *Contagion*, by the laying on of hands, but
only another of thefe Obftacles, which make
the Race of Life fo agreeable a Purfuit. They
exift to fupervife our Doctrines, and find them

unfcriptural, to controul our religious Practices, and forbid their Continuance, thus enabling us to *fnatch a fearful Joy* while we are about 'em: in short, to give the Chriftian Profeffion that Spice of Martyrdom, which it has fo forely lacked fince the Abolition of the *Amphitheatre*. However falutary this Interference be, it is plain that it is of the nature of a Luxury; and we shall, therefore, be content to forgo the enjoyment of it, if the *Non-conformifts* should demand the Sacrifice as a Condition of Re-union with themfelves.

I conceive, then, that within a few years from the prefent Date, the Divifion of Chriftians into Sects for purpofes of Worship will have utterly difappear'd, and we shall find one great United Proteftant Church exifting throughout the civiliz'd World. I would not deny but there might be fome few Difficulties of Adjuft-ment attending the Venture; as, that the *Fifth Monarchy Men* might withhold their Affent from the Scheme, unlefs we would all make it a matter of Doctrine, *That the laft Judgement is to be prefently expected*; which knowledge would caft an intolerable gloom over the more part of our Pleafures, and create a lack of Publick Confidence on the *Exchange.* But I cannot doubt, upon a little cool Reflection, we should rid ourfelves of thefe fanciful *Megrims* of fect-arian Particularity; and there is gain to be shewn on the other fide; for example, it may be anticipated the *Seventh Day Adventifts* will demand the Obfervance of *Saturday* as well as *Sunday* as a Feaft of the Church; and we shall thus have two days inftead of one in every feven on which we can lie abed till Noon, over-eat ourfelves, go out driving in the Country, and dine away from Home under colour of fparing trouble to our Domefticks.

There is fome doubt in this connection, whether or not the churches of *Ruffia* and *Greece*, arrogantly ftyl'd *Orthodox*, can have any part in the Church of the future. Their very Title is, it muft be confeff'd, moft horrid and repellent to our ears; for how can a man pro-claim his own Tenets to be orthodox, without thereby implying, That other People's Opinions are lefs likely to be true, than his own? We muft have no more of this; I leave it to them-felves to pitch upon a new defignation, with the Suggeftion that they would do well to alter their prefent Style to that of *Symphorodox*, which is to affert no more, than that they find their own Doctrines helpful. As to our old Quarrel

about the Claufe *Filioque*, it will clearly have
difappear'd at the time of which we fpeak:
for, as Tradition avers that the *Apoftles*, when
they firft form'd a Creed, did not all profefs it
together, but each fupply'd his Contribution,
Peter leading the way with *I believe in God*, fo
in this new Church nobody will be expected
to recite the whole Creed, but only fuch Claufes
as he finds relish in; it being anticipated that,
with good Fortune, a large Congregation will
ufually manage in this way to recite the whole
Formula between them. And indeed thefe
Oriental Chriftians already enjoy to the full, in
Ruffia at any rate, one of the moft bleffed Privileges of our own Church, which is, to have their
religious affairs entirely controul'd by the
State; and this will prove undoubtedly a great
Bond of Union, when the *Greeks* have been
induc'd to affign the fame Pofition in the Management of their Religion to the *Soldan* of
Turkey, as the *Ruffians* affign to the *Czar*.

But it is not to be fuppof'd that fuch an
Arrangement can be enter'd into without fome
Undertaking from the Eaftern Churches to fet
their own houfe in order: to translate, for
example, their *Liturgy* into the modern Ver-
nacular Tongue; or at leaft to provide that it is,

like our own, not more than three hundred
years out of date: to difpenfe with all Mum-
blings, Bobbings, Bowings, Shutting and Opening of Doors, Kiffings, Gefticulatings, etc.; to
put all their *Ikons* high up on the wall, fo as
to deftroy all peril of Worship; and, finally, if
they cannot but let off Fireworks on *Eafter
Day*, (as their prefent beaftly Cuftom is), to
make fure that they do it only for Purpofes of
Illumination.

Thus it may be hop'd we shall complete the
Reunion of all Chriftians: the Confiderations
fo far brought forward are fo obvious and plain
to all Men of Senfe, that I am well-nigh
asham'd to have dwelt fo long upon them; the
Queftion to be raif'd in the prefent Treatife is
rather, whether we do right to confine thefe
beneficent Operations to the Chriftian or *Trini-
tarian* Sects only, or whether we cannot advan-
tageoufly extend them to other religious Syftems
which have, till now, from a lack of proper
Refleftion, been held to be incompatible with
Chriftianity. And here I do not refer to the
Unitarians; for it is to be fear'd that if thefe
Perfons have gone out of their way to feparate
themfelves from the other Sects on the Ground
of a Doftrine fo little taught in our Church,

and fo little believ'd in, as that of the *Trinity*, they muft be a pettifogging, cantankerous fet of fellows, that prize their own Opinions too highly, to become Parties to our Policy of Re-union. But where Difagreement from ourfelves about the Nature of God arifes, not from any wilful Spirit of Diffenfion, but from Difference of early Training or national Tradition, nay, of Climate, Atmofphere, and geographick Con-ditions; where there are people in the World, who have enjoy'd fo little the Advantages of our modern Enlightenment, as to be unaware that it is not Religion, or Patriotifm, but only the profpect of commercial advantage, that juftifies a Nation in going to War; there, I would humbly venture to urge, there may ftill be hopes of a good Underftanding, when a few Scruples have been remov'd, and a few Doubts explain'd away.

It was cuftomary with our Anceftors, to defignate *Mahomet* by the title of *The Falfe Prophet*. A more modern and more temperate Judgement will not allow us to contend further, than that he was unduly pofitive in his Affer-tions. And there is this to be faid for him at leaft, that he was a good, found *Proteftant*; and that his quarrel with the debaf'd Church

of his Time was mainly about its heathenish
Mariolatry, and the unduly ſtrict views it held
about *Marriage*; all which should make us
conceive a ſympathy and Reſpect for him, as
in ſome ways the Forerunner of our own *Reformation*. Further, it cannot be deny'd, that the
Mahometans admit the hiſtorical truth of many
of thoſe Facts, upon which the Chriſtian Religion
is, or was until the laſt half-century, ſuppoſ'd
to be founded. True, they have hitherto failed
to inveſt the Facts with the ſame theological
colouring we are accuſtom'd to put on them,
and it muſt be confeſt they show a certain
Reluctancy to avow the moſt elementary Articles
of our Faith. But is this Difficulty final? Let
five *Chriſtian*, and five *Mahometan* Theologians
be cloſeted together for a week to diſcuſs theſe
controverted Doctrines, the Chriſtians explaining to their leſs enlighten'd Co-aſſeſſors what
ſenſe ſuch Doctrines are really meant to convey;
and I for one shall be vaſtly ſurpriz'd if, at the
end of the week, the Mahometans are not
prepar'd to accept *the Athanaſian Creed* in the
ſame ſenſe, in which it is maintain'd by ſome
of the moſt highly-plac'd Eccleſiaſticks of our
own Country.

It is, I apprehend, in Matters of Diſcipline

rather than of Doctrine we shall need a certain amount of *give* and *take* before our Differences can be fettled. Chriftian Men are accuftomed to be content with one Wife, and even in *America* with one at a time; Whereas in *Turkey* he would be thought a very chicken-hearted Husband who had not endow'd four Ladies fimultaneoufly with his own Surname. This might feem to be an irreconcilable Difference of Principle; but fortunately, where Numbers are concern'd, Mathematicks provides us with a ready Solution of the Difficulty, by the Method of Averages. Nor does it need the brain of a profound Scholar to determine, that in the Church of the future we shall all be confcientious *Bigamifts*; thereby avoiding at once the Expence of a *Harem*, and the Monotony of our prefent European Syftem. We shall alfo obviate at one blow the difficulty of finding Wives in *Baghdad*, and the difficulty of finding Husbands in *Balham*. We shall, of courfe, adopt at the fame time the Mahometan Rule, by which a Man may at any time turn his Wife out of doors, upon finding her difpleafing to himfelf, and take a new one, modifying it only fo far, as to extend the Privilege equally to the Wife, as to the Hus- band: in this Way we shall meet a long-felt

Demand on the part of the lower Claſſes in our Country, as well as recognizing an exiſting Practice in the caſe of their Superiors in Social Rank. At the ſame time, we shall abolish thoſe accounts of Divorce Court Proceedings in our News-sheets, which are admitted by everyone to be injurious to Publick Morals.

The ſame Principle will naturally rule our Diſpoſitions about the ſacred Hierarchy. Mahometans, as well as Chriſtians, have their ſeveral Grades of Clergy, and it is to be ſuppoſ'd that we should avoid all invidiouſneſs and Suſpicion of Favouritiſm here, if we call'd the Miniſters of the new Church alternately, according to their Rank, by Weſtern and Eaſtern Deſignations. Thus, for example, we might call them (in deſcending Order):

Archbishops
Pashas (correſponding to *Bishops*)
Archdeacons
Mullahs (correſponding to *Rural Deans*)
Incumbents
Hadjis (correſponding to *Unbeneficed Clergy*).

The Services in our Churches (or *Moſques*) would be characteriz'd by a like Spirit of Accommodation. It would be plainly impoffible, to ask Chriftian men to remove their Boots on entering the Building, like the *Mozlems*; but we could make a point of having a fubftantial *Mat* at the door, fo that they could at leaft wipe them; and it would be a pretty Conceit to have the Word, *Salve*, worked on the Mat, in token of our readinefs to welcome all, whatever their Opinions, to Publick Worship. On the other hand, Reciprocity demands, that we should not put any Yoke on the Confcience of the Oriental, by infifting on his taking off his Turban: we should expect him inftead to carry in his Hand a fecond Hat, (preferably a Silk one), fo that when he reach'd his Pew he might not be without fomething to pray into.

Some diffenfions might be expected to arife, about the Reading of the firft Leffon. It is an unfortunate mark of the Barbarifm which ftill triumphs in the Eaft, that the Mahometans have a very confiderable Refpect for their Sacred Book, the *Coran*; and treat it with a Reverence, which our Weftern Enlightenment has long outgrown. Our plea is, that fince we have nowadays fo little ufe for the *Old Teftament*, Readings from the *Coran* should be fubftituted for it in Divine Service. And if any man object, that this might lead to a fuperftitious

Belief in the Facts therein allegd'd, I would point out for his Comfort that in a very short Time that Critical Study will come to be expended on the latter Book, which has hitherto inveftigated the former, with fuch happy Refults; and confequently within twenty years' time we should be in no more danger of giving Credit to the Miracles of *Mahomet*, than we are in now, of ftomaching the Hiftory of *Joshua*.

It is a degraded Practice of the Mahometans, at certain fix'd hours of the day to bring out a little praying-carpet, and kneel on it with the Face turn'd Eaftward, to engage in Prayer. It is manifeft that any Chriftian man would fooner die than be feen at his Devotions, unlefs it were at the time of Publick Service. This Cuftom, then, would of Neceffity be difallow'd, efpecially as in great Cities it would have the effect of continually obftructing the Traffick. But if any felt it difficult to break themfelves of this untidy Habit, I would not deal harshly with them; rather, they should be fuffer'd to carry about a fmall Joint-ftool, and be allow'd thus to meditate in any of the lefs thickly populated Diftricts, under colour of admiring the Scenery. But this is not all: for the Mahometans obftinately infift, when performing fuch Devotions, on turning towards the Eaft, that is, towards the *Sun-rifing*; towards the *Beginnings* or *Origins* of Things, in short, towards the difpiriting Recollection of the Paft. This, (thank God!), is not our way in *Europe*; if any of us should be fo ftrangely affected, as to want to pray in one Direction more than another, it would certainly be towards the Weft, the Land of the *Sunfet*, the glorious Profpect of the remote Future, which, is by all accounts, to be a time of great Happinefs, Virtue, and Profperity. We should fubftitute for *Orientation*, what we might call *Occidentation*; and addrefs ourfelves, not towards *Mecca*, but towards *Chicago*. The fpirit of our religious Compromife thus plainly demands, that every fuch Devotee should carry a *Compafs* about with him; and when the time came for his fuperftitious obfervances, face as nearly as poffible in the direction of the *Magnetick Pole*.

There is another Cuftom prevailing in Mahometan Countries, of fuch doubtful Advantage that we could not agree to conform to it without earneft Confideration; I mean, the Cuftom by which people are woken in the Morning by a Fellow bawling out from the Top of a *Minaret*, to the Effect (unlefs my Memory plays me

falfe) that *Allah is great*. It will feem shocking
to minds habituated to our Weftern Standards
of Tafte, that thefe *Muezzins*, as they are call'd,
should give a Pronouncement fo public to fo
controverfial a Statement. We could not allow
it; for it would manifeftly caufe the most
grievous Diftrefs of Confcience to any *Atheist*
or *Agnoftick* who happened to be within Ear-
shot. Yet is fomething to be faid for the Practice in general Outline; who has not wished,
as he turn'd over in bed at eight of the clock
on a Sunday morning, that there were fome
lefs noify means of awakening a few devout
Women, than making a great *Clanging of Bells*,
as if the whole City were afire? Would it not
be well to introduce the Muezzin into our
Church-towers, and at the fame Time to fee to
it that his Announcement was both lefs provoca-
tive, and more appropriate; that he should
either shout out, *The early Bird catches the Worm*,
or, if he were mufical, even intone to fome
fimple Anglican Chant the Words:

> *Early to Bed, and early to rife,*
> *Makes a Man healthy, wealthy, and wife?*

There are befides one or two particular Sects
among the Mahometans, who might give us

Trouble; as the dancing *Dervifes*, who infift upon making Dancing into a fort of religious Ceremony. We should have to shew thefe very plainly, that the exercifing of the Soul is one thing, and the exercifing of the Legs another. It might even be well to forbid their executing any Dance except the *Ruffian* ones; if they only practif'd thefe, it would fpeedily rid their Dancing from any Affociation of Religion, or even of Morality.

There are the *Affaffins*, too, who hold it to be juft and lawful to kill a man in virtue of a Difagreement about Religion, and did lately murder a man very horribly in the city of *Paris*. Yet thefe should be furely treated, not as publick Enemies, but as erring Brethren: that is, they should be admitted to full Communion, but we should lofe no opportunity of advertifing them of the Difadvantages of their peculiar Tenets, by means of preaching to them in Sermons: reminding them, I mean, that the practice of Murther frequently begets dangerous confequences for the perpetrator of it, by the eftablishing of *Blood-feuds*; and (taking even a higher ground) that where the practice becomes common it creates a general Uncertainty about the Tenure of Life, and renders the

Maintenance of publick Peace and Order a far more difficult affair than it would otherwife be. Doubtlefs in a very short time they would have learn'd to take a more lenient view of doctrinal Irregularities.

There is one Obftacle to Reunion with the Mahometans ftill remaining, which I confefs at firft fight feems wholly infuperable; viz., that the Mahometans hold it finful and unclean to eat the Flesh of the Pig, or to drink fermented Liquours. And though our Countrymen might be prevail'd upon to abandon whatfoever else in the interefts of Peace, there are two Privileges they will never reliquish except at the Sword's point, and namely, *Bacon* and *Beer*. Such practical Confiderations as thefe mean very much more, to a bufinefs-like Nation fuch as we are, than any abftract theory or any matter of ecclefiaftical Principle. Yet even here there is a *Via Media* to be thought upon, which I very earneftly recommend to the Attention of all thofe who have the beft Interefts of Religion at heart. Would it not be poffible to add a Rubrick in the *Book of Common Prayer*, following immediately upon the Rubrick which directs Abftinence on *Fridays*, and Fafting during the forty days of *Lent*, to this effect: "And note.

" that in no circumſtances whatever is it per-
" miſſible on any Day of the Year to eat Bacon,
" Ham, Pork, or Sauſages, or to drink any kind
" of Fermented Liquour; and if the Curate find
" his People ſo doing, he ſhall preſent them to
" the Bishop as contumacious Sinners and
" rotten Members of the Church of Chriſt."
This will ſurely be calculated to eaſe the Con-
ſciences of our Eaſtern Brethren, ſince it will
ſhew them clearly what the Mind of our Church
is upon this matter; whereas on the other hand,
we ſhall have no Scruple at all about the eating
of the Pig, but will continue to eat our Pork
Chops on every Day in the Year, with the ſame
Aſſurance as we eat Mutton on all *Fridays*: in
ſhort, no one will be at all affected in his manner
of life, except a few ſcurvy *Highchurchmen*, who
impiouſly try to gain Merit in the ſight of
Heaven by obſerving theſe and other like Ordin-
ances impoſ'd by the Founders of our Church,
inſtead of contenting themſelves with a ſpiritual
Faſt, which is far more acceptable to God, and
far leſs prejudicial to the Digeſtion.

This ſame Preſcription would, it is clear,
vaſtly leſſen our quarrel with another religious
Sect—I mean, the ancient People of the *Jews*.
Altho' it is to be doubted, whether the ſtubborn

Prejudices of this Nation would be wholly
fatiffied, even by fo fignal a mark of our Deter-
mination to facrifice everything in the caufe
of Unity. Yet I would not defpair, even here,
of fome better Underftanding. For myfelf, I
cannot praife the Suggeftion of my friend *Dr.
Honeybotham*, that we should endeavour to bring
them to a more Chriftian mind, by explaining
to them (what is now prov'd to the fatiffaction
of all our Scholars) that the Law was not given
to Mofes by the difpenfation of Angels upon
Sinai, but rather botch'd together by an ignorant
fellow, who had nothing better to do, at the
time of the Babylonish Captivity : that it is no
bufinefs of ours, to conform ourfelves to the
fanciful Scruples begot in the brain of fuch an
one by an attack of the fpleen. This whole
Propofal has an Air of *Propagandifm* about it,
which can commend it very little to the Enlightenment of the prefent Age, fince it might be
mifconftru'd into a Declaration, that one
man's religious Opinions are in fome way better
than another's.

It would be more congruous with the Principles on which we have hitherto proceeded, if
we would undertake to make further Concef-
fions on our own part. It is a Commonplace

of Theologians in thefe Days, that in all cafes
of Schifm and Divifion among Chriftians either
Party is right in what it *afferts*, and wrong in
what it *denies*.   And it is plain that in the firft
great Schifm of the Chriftian Church, an
account of which is fet down in the fifteenth
chapter of the *Acts of the Apoftles*, the denials
were all on *Saint Paul's* part, and the affirma-
tions on the part of his Adverfaries.   Nor am I
afraid of any Taint of Unorthodoxy, when I
humbly fubmit the Propriety of refcinding the
Decrees of the firft Council of *Hierufalem*, as
we have to all intents already refcinded thofe
of *Chalcedon*, *Ephefus*, *Conftantinople*, and *Nicea*.

It may be thought by the carelefs Obferver,
that we shall have even lefs difficulty in arrang-
ing our terms of Peace and Amity with the
Religions of the further Eaft, as *Buddhifm*,
Brahmanifm, and the like.   For already in our
own time we fee many Men and Women of
Fashion shewing a Tendernefs for the myftical
Doctrines of thefe Sects, keeping *Mahatmas* inftead of Domeftick Chaplains, and cultivating
the Inner Life fo far as the Purfuit does not
interfere with Pleafure, Wealth, and the Enjoyment of polite Society.   Already we fee *Ganges*
flowing into the *Medway*, and it is the part of

every philofophick Mind to difcern thefe Signs
of the Times. For we are all accuftom'd to
comfort ourfelves with the reflection, *Magna
eft Veritas, et praevalebit*; is it not then plain,
that the Prevalence of any Idea is the Meafure
of its Truth? Thus it might well be thought
that all this cult of Oriental Poetry, and Con-
juring, and Fortune-telling, which is now only
practif'd by *Miftrefs Chloe* in her Clofet, muft
contain fuch a Groundwork of Truth as to be
like to commend itfelf, in a few years, to *Dry-
afduft* in his Study. There are, indeed, very
comfortable Doctrines to be found in thefe
Syftems; as, That what a man is, is condition'd,
for the moft part, by what he was in a previous
Incarnation : this quits us of much moral Refpon-
fibility ; and there are not many Men fo fenfitive,
as to feel bound to defend the Honour of a
former Self. And again, that all Exiftence tends
ultimately to Annihilation; which profpect is
a deal more comforting to moft of our *Univerfity
Profeffors, Merchant Princes*, and *Company Pro-
moters*, than anything which was promif'd them
by traditional Christianity.

But it is to be obferv'd, that all thefe Doctrines reft on a moft difquieting *Major Premifs*,
very much adher'd to in the Eaft, *viz., That all*

Matter is evil. Such a pofition will hardly commend itfelf to the Thinkers of our Time. For, if Matter be evil, how can it be that among an enlighten'd People like ourfelves, as is very obvioufly the cafe, the Exploits men can achieve with their Fifts, their Feet, or their Mufcles are far more anxioufly recorded and read of than any Activity of their Brains? That we undergo Exercifes every Morning for the perfecting of our Bodies, and never reflect, from one week's end to another, upon the cafe of our Souls? That we feek bodily Health by every poffible means, and plead it upon every poffible Occafion as an Excufe for our Derelictions? That our Eating and Drinking become every day the fubject of more anxious Cogitation? That the getting of Riches is our Paffion from Birth, our ruling Principle in Marriage, and our only Hope for the Refpect of Pofterity, after our Death? All thefe Confiderations will prove to the fatisfaction of any Philofopher, that if Chriftians have given up every other Article of the Creed, we have ftill a lively Hope in the Refurrection of the Body.

How then are we to come to any Agreement with thofe, who openly profefs that the Body is fomething to be neglected and mortify'd, and that Matter is an evil? I anfwer, *That where there's a Will there's a Way*; and that if we will only confent to admit, for the fake of Charity, that all matter is evil, we can quite eafily fafeguard ourfelves againft any untoward Confequences that might follow from the Doctrine, by adding, That it is a neceffary Evil. The Horrours of War, Poverty, and ill-paid Labour; the Delays and Expence of the Law; the Partyfyftem; the Licentioufnefs of the Prefs; the unequal Diftribution of Stipends among the Clergy—thefe and a hundred other fuch Features of our Polity we all confefs, with one voice, to be evils; but we go on to add, *That they are neceffary evils*, meaning thereby that the Speaker (for one) has no intention of moving a Finger to amend them. If this were clearly underftood, I cannot fee that we should be much the lofers by the adoption of an Eaftern way of thinking.

Yet, God forbid that we should encourage in our own Country any of thofe barbarous Inftitutions, by which thefe benighted *Enthufiafts* attempt to rid themselves of the Body, and its very agreeable Incumbrances; as, by the Inftitution of *Monafteries*, which have made the Religion of the *Buddhifts* almoft as much fufpect as the corrupt Church of the Middle Ages, and,

in fact, little better than it; or by allowing
crack-brained Fellows call'd *Fakirs* to fit by
the Road-fide with no vifible Means of Sub-
fiftence, begging their Bread, fcantily cloath'd,
and afflicting themfelves with lying upon Beds
of Spikes, as if they would rebuke the more
Common-fenfe Manners of the Paffers-by. We
might indeed allow them to ask for Money, if
they would proffer Laces and Almanacks in
Return for it, and fo conform to the Regulations
of the *Police*; but *Spike-beds* I would have
altogether forbidden: and as for the Monks, if
they would not come out again into the World,
I would shut them up for their lives in Mad-
houfes, to cure them of this arrogant craving
for Silence, Confinement, and Solitude.

"But," fomeone will urge "if we hope to
" perfuade thofe who at present difagree with
" us to forgo their fuperftitious Practices for
" the fake of Reunion with the *Church of*
" *England*, we are furely tranfgreffing outfide
" the range of practical Politicks into fanguine
" and vifionary hopes, not likely to be realiz'd.
" If the Buddhifts could be fo far prevailed
" upon, is there not fome profpect of Reunion
" with the *Idolators*, *Fetish-worshippers*, and
" Believers in *Mumbo-Jumbo*; nay, even with

" the *Papifts* themfelves? " And here, I conceive we have arrived at the very Pith of our
prefent Contention. We have much to look for
from the gradual foftening Influence of Time,
from the Progrefs of civiliz'd Ideas, and the wider
Diffufion of Knowledge. And I (for one) am
fo perfwaded of the Miffion of our Church to
unite all the Religions of the World under its
own aufpices, that I do not hefitate to affert
what may feem at firft fight a very diftafteful
Poffibility, namely, that at fome time it will be
our Duty to confider on what terms we fhall
accept the Submiffion even of the *Church of
Rome*. And I would beg of my Readers, not to
be unduly prejudic'd beforehand ; but to take
a lenient view of the abominable Hiftory of
that Inftitution, and as far as poffible to reconcile themfelves to the Profpect of a clofer Relation with thofe, who are at prefent tainted by
the Infection of its impious Tenets.

I know we are commonly told, That this
will never be achiev'd, by Reafon of the
Extreme Obftinacy and Perverfity of this Sect,
which will never allow them to come to any
Conditions. But this Obftinacy, I apprehend,
is nothing elfe than the Confidence of Numbers :
they are at prefent a pretty numerous Body ;

and they will foon be brought to fee Reafon
when they find their own Adherents becoming
rarer every day. That this will fpeedily happen,
Science itfelf gives us warrant to avow; for
we know now that all Survival in the World is
a *Survival of the Fitteft*, and that two Inftincts
chiefly make an Organifm fit to furvive, namely
the *Will to Live*, and the Defire to propagate its
Kind. The *Church of Rome* pays the higheft
Veneration to *Martyrs*, and to *Celibates* or
Virgins, thereby attefting its contempt for thefe
two great Inftincts, which alone enable a Race
to perfift; it might, therefore, be allowed to
become extinct by the force of its own ignorant Delufions; but I hold it a more charitable thing to arreft this Decline, when it has
once fairly fet in, and invite the Survivors,
many of 'em good enough Fellows at heart,
into the all-embracing Unity of our National
Eftablifhment.

True, hitherto thefe Symptoms of Decline
have been flow to manifeft themfelves, and it is
even alledg'd that *Popery* is on the Increafe in
certain parts of the World, notably in our own
Ifland, in *America*, in *Auftralia*, in *France*, and
in *Holland*. But it is not to be fuppof'd, that
any fuch obferv'd Augmentation of Numbers

is due to Converfions; on the contrary, it has been repeatedly prov'd, That nobody is ever converted to the Roman Catholick Religion; in *England*, *America*, and *Auftralia* the whole caufe of Increafe is the Immigration of *Irishmen*, and it cannot be doubted but that a few more Statifticks would show to everybody's fatisfaction, that *Irishmen* are emigrating in very great quantities both to *France* and to *Holland*. Thefe melancholy Facts bear Teftimony both to the Prolifick Character of a Race, which can thus ftock five Countries with *Papifts* from year to year; and alfo to its fingular Obftinacy and Bigotry, in that it carries its Religion about with it, like a part of its Luggage, and muft needs attempt to tranfplant it into an alien Soil, where it was never meant to flourish. Such opinionated Arrogance muft be firmly dealt with; and I would therefore fuggeft, in the interefts of the Reunion of Religions, that upon his Conqueft of Ireland our great Commander Sir E——— C———, should put all *Papift* Children to the Sword, and we should make it a criminal Offence for the future, that any *Papift* should be allowed to marry, or have Iffue: the Offence itfelf to be punish'd with Death, and the refulting Iffue to be expos'd on some Hill-side, left it should grow up infected with the gross Superstition of its Parents.

The Hibernian *Hydra* thus amputated, the remaining *Papists* of the World, seeing their Numbers daily dwindle and decrease, would speedily come crying to us for Admission; and it is here that I would appeal to my Countrymen not to use any undue harshness in receiving their Allegiance. I would not, I mean, altogether treat their Orders as null and void, but only degrade their Clergy by a single step in the Hierarchy; their Bishops to count as Priests, their Priests as Deacons, their Deacons as Layreaders. Nor would I extract from these, by way of a Declaration of Loyalty to our Church, anything more than an Affirmation of general Dissent from the Doctrine contain'd in the *Thirty-nine Articles of Religion*. The *Pope* himself I would allow to take rank as a retir'd Missionary Bishop, thus leaving him the *Insignia* of Power without any Sphere in which to exercise, or Income with which to abuse it. The *Cardinals* I would disperse among the Common-rooms of *Oxford* and *Cambridge*, where they could exercise to the full their Talent for Intrigue without having any serious effect, for

good or ill, upon the Deſtinies of the Nation.
In Diſcipline, Doƈtrine, and Devotion, we should
of courſe compel our newly-returned Prodigal
Brethren to conform entirely to the *Book of
Common Prayer*, and, for fear of any Recrudeſ-
cence of ſuperſtitious Orthodoxy among us as
the reſult of their Incluſion, take an Oath of
them that they unfeignedly disbeliev'd all the
Scriptures of the Old and New Teſtament.

I cannot apprehend any grave conſequences
following from ſuch a courſe of enlighten'd
Charity upon our part; and if any should ſtill
have ſcruples about the Wiſdom of it, I would
mention that the ſum of money we should add
to our Revenues as well by the increaſ'd Sale
of *Bibles*, *Prayer-books*, and *Hymn-books*, as by
the proceeds of the diſmantling of *Cathedrals*,
Churches, and *Monaſteries*, would amply ſuffice
to form a Fund for a publick Training of
Athletes.

The Differences at preſent exiſting between
the various Perſons who believe in a God being
thus happily ended, we should be the more
free, finally, to conſider the Problem of Reunion
with the *Atheiſts*. And here it is to be notic'd,
that whereas the Seƈtaries of one Religion differ
from thoſe of another over a whole Multitude

of Points, as Niceties of Ritual, Quibbles of
Doctrine, Forms and Postures in the Recitation
of Prayer, etc.; in the Cafe of the *Atheists* we
have only one single Quarrel to patch up,
namely, as to whether any God exifts, or not.
If we could but eafe their Confciences on this
matter, it is clear they would have no difficulty
in accepting our Forms and Fashions of Worship, having no inherited prejudice in favour
of any other.   There would be no ftraining at
Gnats, if they could but be brought to fwallow
the *Camel*.   I fubmit it, therefore, with all
deference to our Theologians, whether they
could not find it poffible to allow, that as God
is Immanent and yet Tranfcendent, fo we cannot fee the whole Truth, but only an Afpect of
the Truth, until we have reconcil'd ourfelves
to the laft final Antinomy, that God is both
Exiftent and Non-exiftent?   We, who are confcious of the Supreme Being as Exiftent, and
thofe others who are confcious of Him as Non-
exiftent, are each of us looking at only one Half
of the Truth, one *Side*, as it were, of the *Shield*;
and we can furely hope that when we have
ftudy'd each other's points of view, and come
to underftand them a little better, by common
Difcuffion and common Worship, we shall all

of us recognize the Divine Governor of the
Univerfe as One who exifts, yet does not exift,
caufes Sin, yet hates it, hates it, yet does not
punish it, and promifes us in Heaven a Happinefs, which we shall not have any Confcioufnefs
to enjoy.

It would be fuperfluous to add, what great
Advantage will be deriv'd from the Abfence
of any religious Diffenfion whatever in the
World; as, that there will be no Divifion
within Families, no Tefts in the appointment
of Ministers, and no religious Matter to offend
the eye in our daily News-sheets. I commend
thefe Confiderations very earneftly to the Attention of the Publick, calling upon them in the
name of Humanity and Progrefs to fee that
this Scheme is carry'd out, whether or no any
of the various Sectaries concern'd like the Propofal made; and not to allow the fact that they
do not happen to have any Religion or any
Morality of their own make them in any way
backward to arrange the moral and religious
Affairs of other People. Thank God, in thefe
days of Enlightenment and Eftablishment, everyone has a right to his own Opinions, and chiefly
to the Opinion, That nobody elfe has a right
to their's. It shall go hard, but within a century

at moſt we shall make the *Church of England* true to her Catholic Vocation, which is, plainly, to include within her Borders every poſſible Shade of Belief, *Quod umquam quod uſquam, quod ab ullis.*

II

ABSOLUTE AND ABITOFHELL

*OR NOAH'S ARK PUT IN COMMISSION,
AND SET ADRIFT (WITH NO WALLS
OR ROOF TO CATCH THE FORCE OF
THESE DANGEROUS SEAS) ON A NEW
VOYAGE OF DISCOVERY*

BEING A SATIRE IN THE MANNER
OF MR. JOHN DRYDEN ON A
NEWLY-ISSUED WORK ENTITLED
FOUNDATIONS

II

ABSOLUTE AND ABITOFHELL

Being a Satire in the Manner of Mr. John Dryden upon a
newly-iffu'd Work entitl'd *Foundations*.

IN former Times, when Ifrael's ancient Creed
Took Root fo widely that it ran to Seed;
When Saints were more accounted of than Soap,
And MEN in happy Blindnefs ferv'd the POPE;
Uxorious JEROBOAM, waxen bold,
Tore the Ten Tribes from DAVID's falt'ring Hold,
And, fpurning Threats from Salem's Vatican,
Set gaiter'd Calves in Bethel and in Dan.
So, Freedom reign'd; fo, Priefts, difmay'd by
    naught,
Thought what they pleaf'd, and mention'd what
    they thought.
Three hundred Years, and ftill the Land was
    free'd,
And Bishops ftill, and Judges difagree'd,
Till men began for fome Account to call,
What we believ'd, or why believ'd at all?

The thing was canvaff'd, and it feem'd paft
   doubt
Much we adher'd to we could do without;
Firft, ADAM fell; then NOAH's Ark was drown'd,
And SAMSON under clofe infpection bound;
For DANIEL's Blood the Critick Lions roar'd,
And trembling Hands threw JONAH overboard.
   Lux Mundi came, and here we found indeed
A Maximum and Minimum of Creed:
But ftill the Criticks, bent on MATTHEW's Fall,
And fetting PETER by the Ears with PAUL,
Brought unaccuftom'd Doctrines overfea
Suggefting rather, *Caeli Tenebrae.*
So, while our Ark let in, through Seams ill-join'd
And gaping Timbers, *Bilge* of ev'ry Kind
Ran to and fro, and like a Drunkard shook,
Seven of the Younger Men compof'd a *Book.*
   Seven Men, in Views and Learning near ally'd,
Whom *Forms* alone and *Dogmas* did divide,
Their Differences funk, in Conclave met,
And each his Seal (with Refervations) fet:
Each in his Turn fubfcrib'd the fateful Scroll,
And ftamp'd his *Nihil Conftat* on the whole.
  Sing, Heavenly MUSE, from high Olympus
    bowing,
Their Names, their Training, and their Welt-
    anfchauung,

Say, why did Magdala,[1] renown'd in Ships,
Withhold the Tribute of *his* dauntlefs Lips,
Who, fetting out the Gofpel Truths t'explain,
Thought all that was not German, not germane:
Whofe queafy Stomach', while it tried in vain
Recorded Miracles to entertain,
Efchewing LUKE, JOHN, MATTHEW, and the reft,
Read MARK, but could not inwardly digeft?
Why did Neapolis,[2] aloof like ASHER,
Withhold—the Name is in the Book of Jasher—
Where, 'mid the Thunders of a boisterous Quad,
He ponders on the Raifon d'Être of God?
Not fuch the Arms, not fuch the vain Defence,
That rallied to thy Standard, Common Senfe.

    Firft, from the Public Schools—*Lernaean* Bog—
No paltry Bulwark, ftood the Form of OG.[3]
A man fo broad, to fome he feem'd to be
Not one, but all Mankind in Effigy:
Who, brisk in Term, a Whirlwind in the Long,
Did everything by turns, and nothing wrong,
Bill'd at each Lecture-hall from Thames to Tyne
As Thinker, Usher, Statefman, or Divine.

[1] The Reverend Mr. J. M. Thompfon, Dean of Divinity at the College of St. Mary Magdalen in Oxford.
[2] The Reverend Dr. Haftings Rashdall, S.T.D., Fellow of the College of St. Mary of Winton, in Oxford.
[3] The Reverend Mr. William Temple, fometime Head Mafter of Repton School; fince Incumbent of the Church of St. James, Piccadilly, in Weftminfter.

Born in the Purple, fwift he chofe the Light,
And Lambeth mark'd him for a Nazirite:
Difcerning *Balliol* fnatched him in his teens,
And mourn'd him, early forfeited to *Queen's*.
His name fuffic'd to leave th' infidious tome
A houfehold word in every Englifh Home:
No academick Treatife, high and dry,
Canvaff'd in Walks round Mefopotamy,
Or where in Common Room, when days are
          short,
Soullefs Profeffors gulp difgufted Port.
" Not from the few, the learned, and the pale "
—So ran his meffage—" we expect our Sale;
Man in the Street, our Publication con—
What matter, if the Street be Askkelon? "

    In Weight not lefs, but more advanc'd in
          Height,
Gigantic ELIPHAZ[1] next hove in Sight:
Who 'mid the Prophets' Sons his Trade did ply
In teaching Wells to blefs and magnify.
The Pomegranate upon His Helm difplay'd
His prebendarial Dignity betray'd:
Magdalen to *Univ.* gave him, and from there
He rapidly achiev'd a wider fphere;

---

[1] The Rev. R. G. Parfons, S.T.B., fometime Fellow of Univerfity College in Oxford; fince Rector of Wells Seminary, in
the County of Somerfet.

Gray Hairs alone he wanted, but for that
Ripe for the Apron and the shovel Hat.
Thofe other Six, in punier arms array'd
Crouch'd in his Shadow, and were not afraid.

Yet fomething marr'd that order'd Symmetry :
Say, what did STRATO[1] in their company?
Who, like a Leaven, gave his Tone to all,
'Mid prophet Bands an unfufpected Saul.
For he, difcerning with nice arguings
'Twixt non-effential and effential Things,
Himfelf believing, could no reafon fee
Why any other should believe, but he.
(Himfelf believing, as believing went
In that wild Heyday of th'Eftablishment,
When, on his Throne at Lambeth, Solomon
Uneafy murmur'd, " Something muft be done,"
When fuave Politenefs, temp'ring bigot Zeal,
Corrected, " I believe," to " One does feel.")
He wish'd the *Bilge* away, yet did not feek
To man the *Pumps*, or plug the treach'rous
    Leak :
Would let into our Ark the verieft Crow,
That had the measlieft Olive-branch to show.
Who has not known how pleafant 'tis to figh,
" Others, thank God, are lefs correct than I "?

[1] The Reverend Mr. B. H. Streeter, Fellow of Queen's College in Oxford, and Canon of Hereford.

From such Conclufion (so men faid) averfe,
A Balaam, bleffing what he dared not curfe,
A Scaeva, raifing Powers he could not quell,
Dragging their Coat-tails, followed ABDIEL.[1]
In Height magnificent, in Depth profound,
Bless'd with more Senfe than fome, than all more
  sound,
Gifted as if with Tongues, were there but wit
Among his Audience to interpret it :
Still, like a clumfy Falconer, he'd untie
Tradition's Hood from Reafon's piercing Eye,
And then complain, becaufe she foar'd too
  high.
So labour'd he, in Devorguilla's Pile,
Jowett's and Manning's views to reconcile :
Beneath his Rule (I quote from Dryden's Rhyme)
" The Sons of Belial had a glorious Time,"
And, when he shook his Fift and talk'd of Eve,
Like Devils trembled, but did not believe.

  With sunnier Faith, with more unclouded
    Brow,
Brilliant ARCTURUS[2] did the Fates endow :
Who cried, as joyfully he bound his Sheaves,
" What I believe is what the Church believes " :

---

[1] The Reverend Mr. N. E. Talbot, Fellow of Balliol College
in Oxford.
[2] The Reverend Mr. A. E. Rawlinfon, Student of Chrift
Church in Oxford.

Yet some might find it matter for Reſearch,
Whether the Church taught him, or he the
    Church.
Corpus had trained him Reaſon's Truth to doubt,
And Keble added Faith, to do without.
What matter, whether two and two be four,
So long as none account them to be more?
What difference, whether black be black or
    white,
If no officious Hand turn on the Light?
Whether our Faƈt be Faƈt, no Man can know,
But, Heav'n preſerve us, we will treat it ſo.

    Yet, leſt ſome envious Critick might complain
The BIBLE had been jettiſoned as vain,
Pellucid JABBOK[1] ſhow'd us, how much more
The Bible meant to us than e'er before.
Twelve *Prophets* our unlearn'd forefathers knew,
We are ſcarce ſatisfy'd with twenty-two:
A ſingle *Pſalmiſt* was enough for them,
Our Liſt of Authors rivals A. & M.:
They were content MARK, MATTHEW, LUKE and
    JOHN
Should bleſs th' old-faſhion'd Beds they lay upon:
But we, for ev'ry one of theirs, have two,
And truſt the Watchfulneſs of bleſſed Q.

---

[1] The Reverend Mr. Richard Brook, Fellow of Merton College
in Oxford.

The laſt, EPIGONUS,[1] but not the leaſt,
Levite by Birth, yet not by Calling Prieſt,
Woo'd coy Philoſophy, reluctant Maid,
To bring her troubl'd Siſter timely aid.
His Views on Punishment what need to tell?
Poor, proctor'd Victims lately knew them well,
His pregnant Logick fill'd their only Want,
Temp'ring EZEKIEL with a Dash of KANT.

Hail, dauntless Mariners, that far outſtrip
Previous Attempts to undergird the Ship!
To you this Rhyme, now falt'ring to its End,
Is dedicated by an humble Friend,
Praying that Providence this Wind may uſe
To puff your Sales, and to confound your Views.

[1] W. Moberley, Eſquire, Fellow of Lincoln College in Oxford.

III

A NEW CURE
FOR
RELIGION

A NEW CURE FOR RELIGION

THE OLD, far-fetched notion of religion, which commended itself for so long to the rude intelligence of our ancestors, has fortunately given way, in our own time, to a more reasonable understanding of it. We find it difficult to think ourselves back into that complexion of mind, which conceived of religious truth as a body of philosophical statements and alleged historical facts; as, that grace was or was not indefectible; that it was Paul and not another who wrote to the Ephesians, and the like. Had such facts been demonstrable, is it not certain that in so many centuries of earnest controversy the common judgement of mankind must have resolved the question with ' aye ' or ' no ' long before this? And could it be credibly maintained that it might be a man's duty to resign his benefice, forgo the comrade-ship of his friends, and find himself a new way of living, merely because he had revised his notions about certain doctrinal points, without abating anything of his general zeal for righteousness? The wonder is, assuredly, not that we should have come to think otherwise, but that so defective an apprehension of religious truth should have so long dominated the superstitious fancy of human kind.

In these latter days, men of emancipated intelligence have set before us a view of the whole question better accommodated to the enlightenment of our times. We are now assured that religion is nothing more or less than an attitude of the mind, or rather not of the mind only but of the whole being, towards it matters not what. We have learned to appreciate the truth that all religiously-minded persons, to whatever sect or philosophy they have given in their names, are all in the last resort at one. Each will have made his own guesses about the nature of things; and each will be prone (such is the frailty of the philosophical temper) to fancy that his own guesses are true for others besides himself, and valid outside the sphere of his own judgement. It is the office of reason to curb these hankerings after dogmatism, and to remind us that only one question about religion really signifies, to wit, whether a man is religiously-minded or no. If he be, what matters it whether he worships a whole pantheon of deities, or denies the existence of any? He is still a religious person; and no amount of argument *pro* and *con* will make him the more or the less so. We can have no certainty about what lies outside the reach of our scientific appliances for learning; what is beyond the observation of sense, what rules the chances of history, what awaits us (if anything awaits us) beyond the grave—all these questions are of inferior dignity and secondary interest. There is only one fact about religion, and that fact is that some men are and some are not religious.

But when we have admitted (because candour obliges us to admit) that the true essence of religion is to be found not in a series of supposed external facts, but in a subjective attitude, a difficulty presents itself which it needs no very penetrating ingenuity to forecast. Granted that this religious feeling exists, which is so beneficial to the humane conduct of life, so gratifying (in certain moods, at any rate) to the emotions, and according to some so essentially noble a part of our nature, how is it that it is so unequally

shared among the human race? That this
man should be better endowed with physical
graces than his fellow, should have a more
penetrating intellect or a better ear for music,
is an inequality we have grown accustomed to,
content to remind ourselves that Fortune is a
capricious goddess. But what are we to say
when we find that this amiable gift of religious-
ness, so useful and   so attractive, especially
in the female sex, is dealt out with an even more
sparing hand, so that, put the best face on the
matter we may, the possession of it is still not
the rule, but rather the exception? Few
thoughtful persons can be strangers to this
kind of doubt.

But the same considerations, until recently,
gave rise to a further and a more serious embar-
rassment. Not only was it apparently impossible
for those to acquire this sense of religion who
were not naturally gifted with it, but it seemed
similarly impossible for one who had been so
gifted to be rid, if he would, of his encumbrance.
For it would be affectation to pretend that
there are not many circumstances in which
the sense of religion may be a handicap to a
man's activities—as, when he wishes to amass
a respectable fortune in the competition of

the open market, when he would write books
that are to be taken seriously by the learned
world, and so forth. In such a situation a
man was powerless : it was often observed, too,
by those who had given themselves up to an
irregular course of living, that even in the
midst of their pleasures they felt some twinges
from the survival in them of a conscience for
which they had no further use—*amari aliquid,
quod in ipsis floribus angeret.* What a strange
commentary it seemed upon the limited capa-
cities of man ! In almost every other field,
science had given us the mastery : to avoid the
occurrence or obviate the consequences of
disease we could numb, atrophy, amputate or
trepan almost every part of our bodies ; yet
for these obstinate questionings of the religious
temperaments there was no alleviation and no
remedy.

Some attempt had indeed been made by our
psychologists to deal with the religious phenomenon as a morbid affection of our nervous
complexions ; and it was hoped that when the
roots of the disability were traced to some sudden
shock or forgotten accident of childhood, the
patient could be weaned away from his religious-
ness by being encouraged to transfer his attention

to healthier exercises of the mind. But the
cures which these psychological doctors claimed
were at best only occasional and partial; and
there was the perpetual danger of unforeseen and
unreasonable relapse. We have ourselves known
the case of an unfortunate young gentleman
who, in the very hour when he was about to
negotiate a most successful stroke of business,
was suddenly revisited by those religious qualms
he hoped to have outlived, and found himself
incapable of profiting by an opportunity which
was not likely to be, and in fact was not, repeated.
The story is but one among a thousand melancholy instances.

It is, then, a timely gift that Doctor Mahu
has brought us in his recent discovery that the
seat of religious feelings lies not only in an
ascertainable, but in an accessible part of our
bodily constitution. We do not propose here
to give any exact statement as to the position in
which this long unnoticed gland is situated, or
the means which are available for its treatment.
Nothing is more undesirable than that unqualified persons should undertake the management of
this business; a matter so important is far better
left in the hands of the Mahu Institute. But
we think it no indiscretion to state that the gland

in question can be extracted, when it is present, by an operation no more painful than the drawing of a tooth, and introduced, where it is absent, by a course of treatment which only inconveniences the patient for a matter of two months.   As Dr. Mahu has wittily observed, *il faut souffrir pour être bon ;* but the sacrifice of a little leisure and comfort is surely not unreasonable in comparison with the very considerable benefit which (for those so minded) the system confers.   The only drawback to the operation as at present practised is that, although the conscience artificially introduced can be extracted again without the least difficulty, the conscience once extracted can never be replaced. Patients, therefore, who apply for the excision of the gland will be well advised to weigh carefully beforehand what is, as far as our present knowledge carries us, an irrevocable step.

It was but reasonable to anticipate that so important a discovery would be followed by hasty demands, from one quarter or another, for legislative action.   In spite of a vigorous opposition, notably from the Bishop of Barchester in the Upper and from Mr. Archdeacon Fearless in the Lower House, Convocation passed a resolution last month praying His

Majesty's Government to 'make this important discovery, so fraught with opportunity and with peril, the subject of their speedy and earnest consideration.' The motion proposed by Dr. Pottinger, that Convocation should appeal for the compulsory introduction of the gland into all children whom nature had not provided with it, at the same time and under the same penalties with vaccination, was summarily rejected. It was very powerfully argued by Mr. Butterforth, in opposition, that this forcible indoctrination with religious principles at an age when the subject of the experiment would be incapable of co-operation, would deprive these children of the opportunity they would otherwise enjoy, later in life, of submitting to the process by their own free choice. No one will doubt the sincerity of Dr. Pottinger's convictions; but his attitude on this occasion was, it must be confessed, unduly combative; and we cannot believe that the publication of his pamphlet, 'England englanded,' will cause the public to entertain a higher idea of his character for prudence and for good taste.

A more lively discussion was aroused by Mr. Stoleby's amendment, which would have the performance of the contrary operation, the removal, namely, of the *glans Mahui*, made illegal. This, he maintained, was tantamount to a kind of suicide, an affirmation which he supported by a good deal of theological rhetoric, very repugnant to the spirit of our times. Dr. Dodgely replied in a very pretty speech, merrily asking Mr. Stoleby *If he would make Calvinists of us all willy-nilly? And was it his will to confirm us all in goodness by means of the civil authority?* Mr. Archdeacon Lomax then proposing that at least the House should put on record its detestation of the practice so alluded to, Dr. Dodgely was up again, and proposed that the resolution should read as follows: *That this House strongly deprecates the excision of the* glans Mahui, *unless very exceptional circumstances make the step necessary.* There were, he said, certain persons, fortunately in this country not numerous, who suffered from what the old authors called Scrupulosity, that is, an extreme morbid timorousness of conscience, such as made the lightest irregularity seem to them to have been sinful. For these people, he said, it was better that the gland should be removed altogether, than that they should run the risk of being put into a strait-waistcoat as Muggle-tonian fanatics. But upon a vote being taken, it proved that a majority of the House favoured Mr. Archdeacon Lomax's proposal without any qualifying clause, and it was accordingly put on record; which in a company of Churchmen is a thing not to be surprised at.

The recommendation to His Majesty's Government, drafted by their Lordships in the Upper House, will more naturally challenge attention. The full text of it runs as follows: ' While on the one hand we heartily welcome Dr. Mahu's discovery, and recognize in it a signal confirmation of those basic truths upon which Christianity rests, at the same time we are of opinion that the indiscriminate use of the opportunities for good and evil thus put in our midst may easily be of more harm than benefit. Grave issues are concerned, and we feel that we should not be doing our duty as the leaders of the Church if we did not call attention, in no uncertain tones, to the importance of them. While it is entirely fitting that men and women of mature judgment and duly qualified experience should decide for themselves, earnestly and prayerfully, whether the presence or the absence of the *glans Mahui* will be more fruitful for good in their lives, it is quite another thing that young people, swayed

as young people too often are by the fashion of
the moment, should take any irrevocable step
at the bidding of their own caprice and upon
their own responsibility. It is not, then, the
use of Dr. Mahu's treatment, but its abuse,
that we respectfully venture to call in question.
In view of these facts, we would urge His
Majesty's Government to make this important
discovery, so fraught with opportunity and with
peril, the subject of their speedy and earnest
consideration.'

Frankly, we think their Lordships have made
a mistake. Englishmen value the civil and
religious liberty so hardly won for them by
Magna Charta and the Act of Protestant Succes-
sion; and they will not readily barter that
liberty for the despotic government of any
body of ecclesiastics, however learned and however well-intentioned. We are glad to find that
the names of two enlightened prelates, the
Bishops of Barchester and of Much Wenlock,
are absent from the list of signatories. We are
fully in agreement with their Lordships that the
indiscriminate use of Dr. Mahu's treatment
may lead to abuses. But it is man's privilege
as a free agent to learn from his mistakes; if
rash counsel should prevail at first, right feeling

will re-assert itself; and it is better that a few should learn the lesson of liberty to their cost, than that the whole nation should be subjected for one moment to the execrable odium of a tyranny.

It was equally inevitable that our Jacobin agitators should interpose in the contrary sense. A resolution lately put forward by certain of these gentlemen proposes that all infants indiscriminately should be made the subject of an inspection within six weeks of their birth, and the *glans Mahui* be forthwith removed from all in whom any traces of it are to be discovered. They support this policy of a new *Massacre of the Innocents* by the specious plea that those at least who were born without the gland will be in a position to have it introduced later in life, in the improbable event of their wishing to do so. The gland, says one of their more reckless spokesmen, must be considered as a morbid growth, and its removal be regretted no more than that of a tonsil or an adenoid. We are sorry that these gentlemen should be content to make merry over a matter upon which many of our fellow-countrymen feel deeply.

No one, it seems, has called in question the value of Dr. Mahu's discovery except the apologists of the Papistical body, who make light of the whole subject. They even profess to have perverted to their own abominable errors a young man that had, but three weeks earlier, had his religion extracted by Dr. Mahu for good and all. Which Dr. Mahu hearing of, very prettily retorted that it confirmed what he had always believed, *viz.* that the superstitions of the Papists had nothing at all to do with true religion.

For ourselves, we are content to think that the benefits derived from Dr. Mahu's discovery will be considerable. It has been frequently observed, for example, that the young and marriageable females of our day, whose taste runs to liberty, short hair, and the following of gymnastic pursuits, do not exercise the same attraction over young men as they did formerly, or at least do not invite them as powerfully to the ordered tranquillity of the married state. The proposition may sound fantastic, but for ourselves we have always inclined to the belief that it is in the *irreligiousness* of our modern young ladies that the fault lies. Cupid is not slow to lurk between the pages of a prayer-book : there is something, at least about the external observances of religion, that is a natural ornament to the female sex, as the scent is to the flower. It would not come amiss, we think, if some of these young ladies should submit themselves to Dr. Mahu's treatment, in the hope of securing for themselves eligible partners and a prospect of assured matrimonial felicity.

The introduction of the gland would, it is clear, be of still greater advantage to the indigent poor. It is but fitting, surely, that those who are less well equipped with worldly goods than their neighbours should find relief and compensation for the inequality in the practice of some kind of religion. It is not infrequently to be observed that the accession of wealth will kill a man's taste for religion, while it increases his opportunities for gratifying his other humane emotions. But the poor have few resources of art, music, or literature open to them, and commonly little skill to appreciate such advantages if they had them. Whereas the religious emotion is of the simplest possible kind, and needs no trained palate to relish the smack of it. It is, consequently, all the more to be regretted that our modern enlightenment should have affected not the rich only but the poor with a kind of queasiness for these crude flavours of religion; and, since the operation

is still somewhat costly to be performed, we think
that some charitable person, who should be
disposed to devote something of his fortune to
the needs of the indigent, might well found an
endowment by which the poor could avail
themselves of Dr. Mahu's treatment gratis. We
mean, of course, by way of introducing the
gland where it is absent : to remove it where it
is present would be clearly undesirable in the
case of those whom an inferiority of station in
life naturally disposes towards Jacobinism and
the impiety which it accompanies or begets.

There is an infinity of other situations (had we
time to mention them all in detail) where it
would be convenient if the sense of religion
could be supplied to one who has it not. Is it
not confessedly a more urgent question than
ever, *what to do with our younger sons ?* And are
we not at the same time constantly assured that
there is a difficulty in recruiting the ranks of
the clergy, more especially from among the
cultivated and the leisured classes? Surely it
is evident that the two problems provide an
answer for one another, if only our younger
sons will go to the trouble of having the gland
introduced. It is true that some expense is involved, but the outlay in this case would more

than justify itself in the long run. But the generality of men would doubtless prefer to get through their youth and early manhood unimpeded by any such scruples as might allay their pleasures or thwart their ambitions, and submit to Dr. Mahu's operation at some time after their fortieth year, when (other delights palling upon them by this time) they desired to live out the rest of their days in that mellowness of old age to which a chastened sense of religion so powerfully contributes.

Meanwhile, the advantages of the contrary operation are so evident as scarce to be worth insisting upon. What a vast deal of perplexity there is in our lives, whether in matters of practical conduct or of abstract speculation, which is born of the effort to reconcile this fact which has come to our knowledge, or this act which we intend to perform, with our notions of religious truth or duty! We are, as it were, compelled to sit out a long musical entertainment, which is so full of discord that it offends the ear at every point. Who, at such a concert, would not willingly lose his ear for music, if the loss of it would make him insensible to the jarring of the instruments upon his senses? And how much more will it be of advantage, in the general conduct of our lives, to be able to extirpate in ourselves that fastidiousness which religion begets in us! If we are not mistaken, there will be a rush from all sides to the Mahu Institute, when the possibility of this emancipation is properly understood by the public. Few except those to whom religion is professionally necessary, will shrink, we fancy, from the operation, provided only that they have money enough to defray the cost of it. And let it not be thought an inconsistency, that the same man should pay Dr. Mahu to obliterate his own sense of religion, and at the same time pay him to instil a sense of religion into his poorer neighbours. For it cannot have escaped observation, that when charitable subscriptions are set on foot for the purpose of building churches in the poorer districts of our great cities, a good half of the benefactions come from those who rarely set foot in a church themselves above once in a twelvemonth.

How readily, hitherto, have we excused ourselves, in avoiding any religious duty which seemed incumbent upon our position or station in life, upon the plea that our physician discountenanced the performance of it! Henceforth, we shall be able to reply to all such

appeals by proclaiming that we have a medical
certificate of irreligiousness.   How often we
have suffered under pious homilies, delivered
to us by ministers of religion or by spinster
relations, appealing to our better feelings ! For
the future, we shall be able to give these expos-
tulators a ready answer : ' Alas ! Sir (or Madam),
you speak too late ! A fortnight ago I had that
in me which might have responded to your
appeal.   Now it is within me no longer ; it is
at the Mahu Institute, preserved (they tell me)
in spirits of wine.   To it you may, more fruit-
fully, address your admonitions—not to this
conscienceless torso which has survived the am-
putation.'   The most inveterate of moralists
might well be checked on meeting with so
singular a rejoinder.

A very horrid doubt has been proposed by
Mr. Clump : *Whether the total extirpation of
religious feeling will not rob our unlawful pleasures
of a great part of their pleasurableness ?*   For, says
he, it is very manifest to all that an urchin at
school will smoke tobacco as long as his usher
forbids it : not deriving any comfort therefrom,
but rather the contrary : yet, so powerfully is
the love of disobedience ingrained in all of us,
that he will take pleasure therein.   So it is, says

the learned author, with acts forbidden by the moral law; if we lacked conscience altogether, such acts would lose a great part of their relish for us, and we should be little better than the brute beasts. Mr. Clump's contentions have hitherto restrained many persons from applying to Dr. Mahu for treatment; but for ourselves, with all respect, we think his apprehensions to be visionary. If the whole human race were to lose its *glans Mahui*, there is indeed reason to fear that they would be well grounded; but this, as we have already shown, is little likely to happen. So long, then, as any considerable part of our fellow-countrymen go about the world fully-glanded, there will always be enough public reprobation of wickedness to impart the necessary tang of guilt to our irregularities : not even blasphemy itself, we take it, will altogether lose its attraction for us, so long as there are pious ears to be shocked.

In conclusion, we may observe that whatever use is made, by whatever proportion of mankind, of Dr. Mahu's treatment, the fact of his discovery will have great advantages for the cause of religion in general. Hypocrisy can flourish no longer, when it needs nothing more than a radiographical inspection of a man's

anatomy to determine whether he be truly
religious or no. Persons who are applying for
positions as private tutors, nursery governesses,
etc., will no longer need to carry with them a
whole sheaf of *references*, when they bear their
testimonials of good conduct stamped upon their
own persons. And, finally, the whole problem
of re-union between the various Christian bodies
will be solved once and for all. No one, we
fancy, will be un-Christian enough to find fault
with the beliefs or the practices of another that
is as completely glanded as himself. Henceforth,
for all Christians, there will be a single gland of
fellowship in which all religious persons (probably not very numerous in all) will be at last
visibly united. Dr. Mahu is too modest a man
to claim for himself the title of a religious re-
former: yet history has her crowns for the
unpretending, and the candid critic must not
be suspected of extravagance when he prognosti-
cates with all the certainty of which such human
prophecies are capable, that this fearless dis-
coverer will go down to posterity with Wycliffe
and Luther, with Hume and Voltaire, as one
of the great liberators of mankind.

IV
THE NEW SIN

IV

THE NEW SIN

THE FIRST advertisement didn't attract much attention. It was quite unclassified, and the advertisement editors, after a single glance, immediately put it down under Theatre Engagements. It ran simply, " Look out for the New Sin : Professor Laileb's remarkable discovery : Satisfaction Guaranteed." Naturally, the public merely supposed it to be the title of a new *revue*, and—already somewhat jaded—awaited the appearance of Press notices. But the next was far more formidable, appearing in the most expensive pages of the daily Press, and in very large letters all over the underground stations : " Professor Laileb's Great Discovery. On Tuesday, September 27 (the date was about a month and a half ahead), Professor Laileb will lecture in the Albert Hall at 3 p.m. on The New Sin, recently discovered by him and now for the first time brought to the notice of

the public.   All seats free."   The mention of
free seats and the Albert Hall made it clear
that the Professor had money behind him, and
was a person to be reckoned with ; he was also
a generous advertiser, and the leading daily
papers lost no time in fishing out all they could
in the way of information and writing him up
as a Silly Season column.   The public, though
gravely afraid (from the use of the word
" lecture ") that this particular form of trans-
gression must be a System, needing (like the
Physical Development and Memory-training
Systems) stern months of self-discipline for its
acquisition, nevertheless pricked up its ears, and
was ready to know all about Professor Laileb
that there was to be known.

This was singularly little.   He was staying
at the Langham, which found its gates uncom-
fortably thronged with enquirers, and its staff
being replaced at an alarming rate by enter-
prising journalists in disguise.   On the rare
occasions when the Professor went out, he was
attended by a horde of photographers, and their
results figured boldly in the illustrated papers
under a variety of titles, of which " Thinking
out Another " and " Professor Laileb at it
again " were among the least sportive.   But

actual information of any interesting kind was hopelessly wanting. Professor Laileb kept regular hours, drank only in moderation, indulged in no mysterious occupations, seemed to partake no more and no less than his neighbours in the more hackneyed imperfections of human nature. Of his origin, nothing was known, nothing revealed to interviewers. The British public, always impressed by a foreign name in matters of learning, and always ready to take the title of " Professor " on trust, without examining the details of graduation, was prepared to accept him at his own estimate. So was the Press, unless we accept the *New Witness*, which was immediately in a position to give the name of the actual street in Vienna where he was born, and the actual synagogue which gave its cast to his early theological training.

On the subject of the Sin itself, the Professor was pardonably reticent. No, it was not a mere by-form or adaptation of any existing sin ; it was not a matter of circumstances or of method that constituted its novelty. It was, he proudly said, as if someone had added a new colour to the rainbow. It reacted properly on all the usual tests of a sin ; it was harmful to society in the long run, it gave a pleasing twinge of regret to the conscience, it definitely lowered the general moral level of its votaries. It was a purely original discovery, not a lost art unearthed from the Renaissance or any other forgotten period. And so Professor Laileb would bow the interviewer out, as mystified as ever, not failing to assure him of the high respect he entertained for the Press as an institution, and the deep conviction he had of its supreme mission as an educative influence

But where interest is sufficiently aroused, lack of precise knowledge makes an agreeable stimulant to speculation. Thus the *Daily Mail*, after its inevitable articles on " Sins of the Century " and " The World's Great Sinners," left the discussion to its readers, who fell upon it eagerly from a variety of standpoints. " A Britisher " wrote from Walthamstow demanding that, in the interests of our all-round supremacy, the secret should not be allowed to travel outside these islands. A certain Mr. Borthwick Stapleton, writing from Newport Pagnell, engineered a crusade against it, which only lasted three numbers. " An anxious Mother " tried to organize a fund for inducing Professor Laileb to keep his mouth shut. " A Sinner of Forty Years' Standing " pooh-poohed the whole

story, and argued that the sin was perfectly
familiar to himself, and as old as the Fall.
Challenged, he professed himself disinclined to
furnish any particulars.   Next day, however,
the Vicar of Much Boosting was almost certain
that its nature had been disclosed to his grand-
father by Lord Chesterfield.   (This led to some
rather irrelevant side-controversies on Memory,
Longevity, and British Sea Power.)   Somebody dreamt that he had discovered the secret,
but forgotten it, and there was a full tide of
letters on Occultism and Thought-transference.
There were proposed Memorials to the Government in favour of the sin and against it, attacks
on Professor Laileb, followed by hasty retrac-
tations, and several Deans earned a reputation
for broad-mindedness by appealing to the
public not to condemn him unheard.

The Times dealt with the matter to everybody's satisfaction in an article " from a Corre-
spondent " on page 11.   The old order—this
gentleman reminded the paper's readers—yields
place to the new, and civilization fulfils itself in
many ways.   It was not in the nature of human
thought to remain stationary, and in the new
order of things that was just dawning (nobody
ever knows why, but it always is) it was fitting

that new sin-forms should replace the old, not by superseding them, but by absorbing them and as it were crowning them with a splendid maturity. There were, and there always would be, old-fashioned people who were disturbed by the removal of old landmarks, and on this as on every other occasion tried to stem the broad current of progress. There was innovation which was innovation, and innovation which was not so much innovation as Renewal. We needed courage and enterprise to adapt ourselves to the new situation as our forefathers adapted themselves to the old. It might be that there would be stress, strain, crisis—even conflict. That would pass; whatever was valuable, whether in the new or in the old, would remain. All that was best always did come as the resultant of conflicting forces. Look at sport, for instance (for the article appeared on the 12th of August, and was headed " The Twelfth " to make the reader think it was about grouse-shooting). On the one side you had the instinct of self-preservation, the will to live: on the other side the ardour of the chase, blinding its votary to all else; and the result? Game for our dinner-tables, a result how little connected with the conscious

motivation of either combatant! So it was
with all human striving and human endeavour;
we always struggled blindly for an ideal, we
did not quite know what, using means that
might or might not have the intended effect,
and the result was always something we had
never envisaged, and, if we had, would certainly not have wished to secure. People talked
of the new sin as a great problem, but there
was only one problem in reality, whether our
generation would rise to the magnitude of the
situation, and strain fearless eyes towards the
ever-receding horizon. This notable document
was everywhere quoted with approval, and was
reprinted as a booklet (in the *Whither?* series)
by the Uplift Publishing Company of New
York.

The more politically-minded of our national
organs were a little at sea as to the bearing of
the discovery. The *Morning Post* naturally
scented Bolshevism in it, and the *Herald* regarded
it as the Mene Tekel of Capitalism, but, owing
to the complete absence of data, it was not found
easy to develop either train of thought. Thus
it was the Sunday papers that chiefly spread
themselves in criticism. For a time, indeed,
these showed a delicacy in approaching the

subject, which gave rise to comment. Some light is thrown on their hesitation by a mysterious visit to Professor Laileb from a gentleman representing " certain important interests," who (if I am rightly informed) offered him a very substantial sum down on condition of his transferring his lecture to 5 p.m. of Saturday, October 1st—an hour which would make it impossible for any report to appear in the evening papers of Saturday. He refused courteously. But no section of the Press—even the modern Press—could have succeeded in boycotting Professor Laileb; you might as well have tried to boycott a total eclipse. And when the Sunday papers did betake themselves to the theme, it will easily be imagined what scope they found in it—what symposia of public men, what personal paragraphs, what sermons by topical divines, what *questionnaires* to theatrical managers, raised and re-raised in every conceivable bearing the mystery of Professor Laileb and his Sin.

The weeklies tended to be unfavourable. The *Spectator*, indeed, showed some signs of hedging, and deprecated any attacks upon the innovator that should be based on mere shibboleths of sect and creed; we were not bound

(thank God !) by all the glosses which the narrow
scholasticism of the Dark Ages had put upon
a particular code of morals issued (probably
in post-exilic times) to a nomad people of
imperfect education. No, we are not to let
the word " sin " frighten us. But it thought
that, in the hopeless bankruptcy of contemporary ideals, it would have been far more satis-
factory if Professor Laileb had devoted his
very considerable researches to the discovery
of a new virtue. The more progressive papers
of the expensive order looked coldly on the
whole business, not because it was sinful or
(Heaven knows) because it was new, but because
it was vulgar in the manner of its appearance
and had aroused popular enthusiasm. The
British Weekly launched out into a series ot
Jeremiads against the discovery, which would
have given Professor Laileb grounds for a score
of libel actions ; but, to the surprise of the
public, he not only abstained from any such
action, but quoted largely from the *British
Weekly's* comment in his now quite ubiquitous
advertisements ; nothing could have drawn
attention in a more gratifying way to the
hopeless degradation of the sin and the hopeless
turpitude of its inventor. But meanwhile *John*

Bull had taken up the controversy, declaring roundly that if Professor Laileb was a rogue, at least he was an honest one, and that all the mealy-mouthed Pecksniffs and Chadbands who beslobbered him with their sanctimonious Pharisaisms were prurient prudes, who were themselves privately guilty of half a dozen vices far more heinous than his. Professor Laileb was furious. He declared himself the victim of a conspiracy, demanded apologies, threatened actions : the article was calculated to damage his reputation and ruin his business. Then suddenly the thing subsided, and *John Bull* never referred to Professor Laileb again.

Meanwhile the public naturally talked of nothing else. Statisticians reported that more bets had been laid on this than on any other event within living memory; the Stock Exchange, in particular, had a most popular sweepstake as to which precept in the Decalogue would prove to be most nearly infringed. Numerous enthusiasts insured themselves at Lloyds' against any possible form of disappointment on September 27th. The theatres languished, even in the provinces ; the managers complained that the public was all out for novelty, and nothing they could do would satisfy it. Even the pictures were unfrequented, since the Professor had sold his film rights to a forthcoming enterprise of his own which described itself as the New Cinema. Money was tight, for he had dropped a hint about floating, in October, a New Syndicate. Parliament congratulated itself heartily on the recess, but a by-election in a Northern constituency looked as if it might be fought on this sole issue. Both candidates tried to hedge by saying that it was not a party question, and neither side of the House had (ha!) a monopoly of these things; but before long both found themselves pledged to expel Professor Laileb from the country, to secure him a peerage, to take the chair at his meeting, to get his meeting stopped, to suppress his discovery, to promote it in every possible way, and to make sure that it was immediately taken over by the Nation. The election was finally decided in favour of a candidate who had once unsuccessfully defended in court a pawnbroker of the name of Laibach.

Ecclesiastical circles viewed the whole affair not, of course, with a personal, but with a thoroughly professional interest. The *Church*

Times, with its keen eye for the latest development, led the way. It even seems to have
hesitated for a moment as to the propriety of
reproducing the great advertisement, but com-
promised in the end by printing it, and coming
out in the same issue with a pulverizing leader,
calculated to extirpate Professor Laileb's sin,
whatever it should prove to be. It warned
churchpeople against attending the Albert Hall
meeting, which could not possibly do good,
and might very well do harm. The Professor's
doctrines were, it appeared, the logical outcome
of Archbishop Cranmer's. It would do good
if Dedication Festival services, occurring about
that time, were specially well attended as a
sort of protest. Accepting a current rumour
that the Professor was a Serbian by origin, it
conjectured that he had been expelled from
his own country as a heresiarch, and deplored
the anomalous state of things which made it
impossible for Convocation to follow the
example of the Serbian authorities. The clergy
of the corresponding school, in their parish
magazines, put down all the trouble to the
weak and ineffective attitude of the Bishops;
why could not the Bishops, at the eleventh
hour, put themselves at the head of a great

movement? But Bishops do not read parish magazines, and (to do them justice) were mostly enjoying a well-deserved holiday.

The Broad Church point of view was perhaps best represented by a thoughtful article from a well-known theologian, Canon Dives. Sin, he argued, was only an upward step in the direction of righteousness, nay, in a sense it was the unformed matter out of which righteousness itself took shape. Innocence which had never experienced and triumphed over sin, was, properly speaking, no innocence at all. By parity of reasoning, the more sins you had become acquainted with and fought with, the more perfect did your innocence become. Professor Laileb, then, in giving us a wholly new sin, was giving us the opportunity of overcoming a wholly new temptation; and, since virtues differ specifically according to the sins they avoid, as temperance, humility, etc., it was plain that he had, consciously or unconsciously, provided us with a hitherto unknown virtue. Canon Dives urged his readers to attend the lecture fearlessly and acquire the new Virtue as soon as possible. What Professor Laileb would have retorted to this charge it is not easy to conjecture, but fortunately the article, being sent to the *Church Quarterly Review*, did not appear until several months after the whole excitement was over. The more old-fashioned leaders of religious thought seem to have pained the Professor a little by their neglect, but the Anglo-Israelite group made up for it by promptly announcing the imminence of the Last Judgement. Professor Laileb was variously identified with the Star Wormwood, the Locusts out of the pit, the First Beast, the Second Beast, the great hail, and each of the three frogs that came out of the mouth of the false prophet. All the interpreters, however, were agreed on one point—that it all showed how plain was the meaning of Scripture, if you only took it in its literal sense.

The Catholic theologians were a good deal exercised over the theoretical aspect of the question. The Dominicans maintained that, if the course of action recommended by Professor Laileb was contrary to any existing precept, divine or ecclesiastical, it was not new; if it was not, it could not properly be called a sin. "The New Sin" was therefore a contradiction in terms. But a school of moral theologians, who perhaps looked forward to new appendices and new cases of conscience, dissented from the verdict; if the sin was all its inventor said it was, there must clearly be something in it contrary to the natural law, and consequently no direct precept on the subject was necessary. Finally, it was generally agreed that the new sin was in all probability only new *quoad nos*, and only a sin *secundum quid*. But the controversy only agitated the pundits; the Catholic public in general was not going to excite itself over a single addition to the numerous existing forms of Satanism.

It was the very up-to-date religions that were more put on their mettle. The Christian Scientists said, of course, that it could not be a sin, because nothing was; it could only be an illusion. Since, however, there was every prospect that it would be a grateful illusion, many of them showed no reluctance to attend the meeting. The Spiritualists naturally had the time of their lives trying to find out from the mediums what the secret was about, but their results were somewhat disappointing. Fifty per cent. of the answers were badly off the point, and the rest largely unprintable without being in the least illuminating; the only at all promising message came from automatic writing, and ran simply, " He doesn't want us to say." Nothing daunted, the Theosophists advertised a lecture on " The true significance of the New Sin " ; their hall only held three hundred, and the crowds turned away from the door beat all previous records. But the lecturer did not get far. She started off by saying that the Laileb discovery, when properly understood, did not involve any external action, and belonged not to the sensible but to the supra-sensible plane. She just got out of the door in time, and the audience contented itself with wrecking the harmonium and two dozen chairs.

Time was now getting on, and these unprofitable speculations began to be over-shadowed in people's minds by the all-important question of how to get a place in the Albert Hall. It was, of course, quite clear that Professor Laileb's audience would not be sympathetic. Nine out of every ten people you met fully intended to go, but it was a mysterious fact that they all went from purely scientific or purely professional motives. The Bar would be heavily represented, in case the New Sin should prove to be also a crime ; doctors were going, in case it should throw

any light on disease; dons, so as to be abreast
of modern thought; schoolmasters, so as to know
what attitude ought to be adopted in form;
business men, to see that their daughters didn't
go; their daughters, so as to show the old thing
that they were not going to be kept in apron-
strings; artists and literary folk of all descrip-
tions, in the hope of deriving inspiration;
actors, so as to study Professor Laileb's manner;
critics, so as to hear what he had to say for
himself—in a word, London had never been
so broad-minded or so conscientious.   The
clergy, of course, simply had to go, for the
sake of their congregations.   Wives meant to
stay at home, but with a certain chastened
confidence that they would get first news from
their husbands.   The only galling part was
the freedom of all the seats.   The prices offered
for reserved seats from various quarters were
(if the accounts given of them are true)
simply fabulous: Professor Laileb was adamant.
His art, he objected, was its own reward; it
should never be said of him that he had opposed
the claim of the less fortunate classes to an
equal share in the ripest fruits of civilization.
Enough for him, he finely said, if he could
contrive to leave the life of a costermonger or

a window-cleaner fuller and richer than he
found it.

But a terrible whisper began to get abroad.
No one knows who started it; it was received
everywhere with incredulity, nay, with ridicule;
nobody dared to assert it as positive fact.
Yet the whisper remained, and finally Professor
Laileb was challenged to allay suspicion. Was
it true—was it thinkable, that he had omitted
to reserve special seats even for the represen-
tatives of the Press? The suggestion, monstrous
at any time, was in this case peculiarly out of
place; for it was no common class of reporters
that had undertaken the duty of transcribing
the momentous speech. Some of the most
prominent figures in journalism, even editors
themselves, had been found willing to sacrifice
their evening in the interests of the public.
Was it true that the Professor had assigned no
special accommodation for these? The answer
came like a thunderbolt. Professor Laileb was
sorry, but he did not feel it to be consistent
with the dignity of his mission to reserve any
seats whatever in the building, except for
himself, his chairman, and three of his most
valued supporters.

Too late, the Press tried to avenge itself.

Not by any undignified outcry; not by attacking the fair fame of the man who had insulted it. But very gradually, very delicately, insinuations began to appear in all the papers suggesting that the Sin was not really so sinful after all. It was an ingenious novelty, no doubt; it would not commend itself, maybe, to our more strait-laced moralists, but as for being actually harmful . . . well, it was a matter of taste. The public must not build its expectations too high; the art of advertisement was one thing, ability to deliver the goods was quite another. And so the chorus of sinister imputations grew in volume, until finally the *Daily Express* broke loose, and in a virulent article, headed " The Dud Sin," challenged Professor Laileb to produce any evidence that his show was better entertainment for an evening than an ordinary music-hall. He did not lose his head; the reply was calm and dignified. He simply deposited the sum of £10,000, pledging himself to hand it over to anyone who, after September 27th, should devise a code of ethics of which the new sin would not be totally subversive.

This brought out official Nonconformity into opposition. Hitherto, the Free Churches had

vaguely hoped that the threatened innovation
was a matter of mere technicalities, something
like divorce law reform. But now firm action
seemed to be indicated, and the wires buzzed
merrily. A good many protest meetings were
held in various parts, and strong resolutions
were adopted, calling on the police, the Watch
Committee, and the L.C.C. to intervene ; even
demanding that Parliament should reassemble.
The children of numerous Sunday Schools took
an oath to abstain from the New Sin before
they even knew what it was. Royalty was
approached ; several Members of Parliament
wrote letters to the *Daily News*. But the
agitation, if it ever had a chance, was too late
in the field ; the public meant to hold that
meeting, if it had to go to Holland for it.

Early in the morning of Monday, September
26th, there was a fair-sized *queue* outside the
Albert Hall. The police moved it on ; it
reassembled. By the middle of the afternoon
there was a picket of horse-policemen, who
kept order with difficulty. There was a thin
drizzle during the night, but thousands under
umbrellas held their own against it. From the
dawning hours of Tuesday, traffic was out of
the question. The Park Gates had to be closed

at several places. All down Knightsbridge you could not see an inch of the pavement. The Langham cut off its telephone communication: it could not cope with the inquiries. The day was fine, but, as it wore on, a threatening bank of cloud rose from the West; the air was electric and overcharged. An aeroplane appeared from nowhere in particular, and gently moulted Anti-New-Sin Society pamphlets. . . .

For my accounts of the proceedings inside the Hall I depend, alas, on hearsay. The doors opened at one o'clock, and the building filled up like a lock in flood-time. There was a band which played ragtime airs, that seemed strangely old-fashioned and pathetic; the meeting was dissatisfied with the effect, and various irrelevant demonstrations rose from different parts of the building, " The Red Flag " mingling inharmoniously with " Round the sacred city gather." Two or three times attendants appeared on the platform, and were applauded by mistake. The cloud-bank mounted higher outside, and the sunlight paled and grew ominous.

Professor Laileb, whom no one has ever accused of disregarding the conventions, was punctual to the minute. He was short, fashionably dressed, slightly grizzled: a suspicion of side-whiskers made him seem vaguely old-fashioned; you would have put him down for a professional man rather than a research student. He looked straight in front of him, as if he took in the whole of that vast audience. His chairman, a most insignificant M.P., intoned the prescribed ritual of oratorical patter —would not keep them long—thought they all knew why they had come there—no introduction necessary—he himself as eager as anyone else to get on to business—he believed in every man having a fair hearing, without committing himself beforehand to all the Professor might have to say—there, he would not detain them any longer.

The shadow of the cloud crept over the last of the windows, and Professor Laileb stood up. There was applause, but it was almost drowned in impatient Hushes.

" The pioneers of any movement," began the Professor, " are proverbially liable to detraction. Habit, lack of initiative, the love of the rut— these factors, so powerful in deterring the individual from stepping outside the beaten path, reflect themselves, in the case of the mob,

in a singular reluctance to see another set foot
on the mountain-track which we have declared
unsafe for our own passage. The dead-weights
which clog all independent human action are
the material we use for stoning the prophets.
I was not unaware, when I began to institute
researches into a branch of science hitherto
comparatively undeveloped, that I was exposing myself in so doing to the opprobrium of
small minds. I am not without experience of
the fate that awaits the innovator. Indeed "—a
smile of singular melancholy passed over the
Professor's features as he said this—" years
ago I lost a very good position myself, simply
through my dislike of always following with
the herd.

" For longer time now than I care to remember, I have been strongly impressed with the
absence of any scientific inquiry into a subject
which interests us all so deeply and concerns
us all so nearly as that of sin. Picture it to
yourselves: the pursuit to which we devote
more than half our lives, for which we are
ready to postpone so many opportunities of
leisure and contentment, so much of our tranquillity of mind; the factor which has so pro-
foundly affected every development of human

history; the ideal which has been the sole inspiration of so much that is most remarkable in the recent literature of Europe—this pursuit, this factor, this ideal, is still neglected everywhere as a subject of organized research. Philosophers have filled libraries with their inquiries into the study of ethics—the problem of how to act rightly; they have never dared to look facts in the face, and, recognizing the hopelessness of a struggle against human progress, resigned themselves to the problem of how we are to act in a manner more accurately, more fully, more deliberately wrong.

" I will not weary you, for the present at any rate, with the history of my early struggles. Suffice it to say that I found myself, after years of endeavour, in a position to add substantially to the opportunities of mankind for developing this most characteristic side of its nature. It will be asked why I determined to choose England, to choose London, to choose this particular building and these particular circumstances, for the disclosure of my results. My reason was simple. I knew that for purposes of publicity London is the world's best centre, and that the thing which impresses it most is a meeting of a half-scientific, half-political character such as the present. As I stand here, I feel that I am speaking through a megaphone to the civilized world.

" I was determined to give the fruits of my study to humanity. If, in all these years, no one had hit upon my discovery by accident, it might well be that the secret, unless I revealed it, would remain for ever unguessed. It did, of course, occur to me to wonder whether my fellow-creatures were worthy of the revelation ; but the doubt did not seriously give me pause. In the case of a boy's education, or in the testing of a confidential servant, we begin by entrusting the neophyte with business of little importance, and advance him further in proportion as he has shown faithfulness and aptitude already. Gentlemen, it seemed to me that the human race, to judge by the use it made of its existing opportunities for wrongdoing, had shown itself full worthy of initiation into a higher degree. Every day I have spent in London, every observation I have made during my brief stay in your city, has fortified me in my opinion and encouraged me to carry out my decision. I studied your legal institutions, your business methods, your ambitions, your pleasures, and said to myself that London

would look back on all this as an age of innocence before I had done with it. My share in
the transformation might be forgotten, history
might be silent about me, but generation upon
generation of your descendants would live by
my precept, perhaps hardly even paying me
the compliment of remembering that it was
wrong.

"And now, let us get to business." The
Professor's voice, which had hitherto been of a
silvery quality, admirable for its rhetorical value,
rang out sharply and crisply at these words like
the crack of a whip. At the same time he
looked round, hostess-like, at his four supporters
on the platform, and these, as by some previous
arrangement, retired by a side door, leaving
the Professor face to face with his audience,
alone on the platform. The light in the Hall
was now still more ominously pallid, and there
was an occasional roll of distant thunder;
everybody in the audience felt, I am told, an
extraordinary sense of close contact with the
distinguished forceful figure that now loomed
solitary in front of them.

"As I said," continued the Professor, "I
had determined to make known my discovery
to the world. I had reckoned on opposition;

for reasons which I need not go into, I had
nothing to fear from that. I had reckoned.
I must say, on incredulity; I was gratified to
find that, on this head, I had done the British
public an injustice. In a word, until the
moment when I came on to this platform, I
thought that I had counted the cost, and was
prepared to go through with it.

"It was only when I looked round on my
audience that I realized something was wrong.
Gentlemen, I regret to say that you are not the
stuff sinners (I use the term in its higher sense)
are made of. You did not come here because
you wanted to do something naughty : you came
here because you wanted to know about something naughty, to get wind of it and be able to
talk intelligently about it before other people
could, to make sure that it should be your
wives who explained it to your neighbours'
wives, and not the other way about. You would
flatter yourselves with being men of the world,
with no nonsense about you, broad-minded
enough to understand the attitude of people
who did not see eye to eye with you. You were
not vicious, as I had hoped, you were just
monumentally inquisitive. And there is about
your inquisitiveness a quality—something I

do not find it easy to define in terms—a quality which is simply revolting to me. Curiosity is the easiest of all sins to punish, for it carries with it its own worst punishment when it is ungratified. Gentlemen, the New Sin is not a mere fraud; I could explain it to you in half a dozen sentences. But I am not going to tell you about it. I shall go back to the place I came from, and leave you to go to hell as best you may with the assistance of those dreary, hackneyed sins whose familiarity almost sickens you of them. Gentlemen, good night."

The wave of a single impulse moved over the vast audience, and swept them onwards, as if they had been drilling for it for weeks, towards the platform. They did not want any New Sin now; they just wanted the old, conventional sin of murder. And then the storm broke, and the hall was suddenly illuminated by a brilliant lightning flash, which showed each man the face of his neighbour, drawn with insatiable hatred. And with the flash, Professor Laileb suddenly disappeared from the platform, and all inquiries (conducted, you may be sure, with the utmost thoroughness and good-will) failed to reveal any clue to his existence.

You blame the public, reader, as the
Professor did, for its inquisitiveness? Truly,
curiosity is the most odious of vices. But,
confess now, when you began to read this
history yourself, had you not a faint hope that,
before reaching the end of it, you would find
out what the New Sin really was?

STUDIES

IN THE

LITERATURE OF SHERLOCK HOLMES

V

STUDIES IN THE LITERATURE OF SHERLOCK HOLMES

IF THERE is anything pleasant in life, it is doing what we aren't meant to do. If there is anything pleasant in criticism, it is finding out what we aren't meant to find out. It is the method by which we treat as significant what the author did not mean to be significant, by which we single out as essential what the author regarded as incidental. Thus, if one brings out a book on turnips, the modern scholar tries to discover from it whether the author was on good terms with his wife; if a poet writes on buttercups, every word he says may be used as evidence against him at an inquest of his views on a future existence. On this fascinating principle, we delight to extort economic evidence from Aristophanes, because Aristophanes knew nothing of economics: we try to extract cryptograms from Shakespeare,

because we are inwardly certain that Shakespeare never put them there : we sift and winnow
the Gospel of St. Luke, in order to produce a
Synoptic problem, because St. Luke, poor man,
never knew the Synoptic problem to exist.

There is, however, a special fascination in
applying this method to Sherlock Holmes,
because it is, in a sense, Holmes's own method.
' It has long been an axiom of mine,' he says,
' that the little things are infinitely the most
important.' It might be the motto of his
life's work.   And it is, is it not, as we clergymen
say, by the little things, the apparently unimportant things, that we judge of a man's
character.

If anyone objects, that the study of Holmes
literature is unworthy of scholarly attention,
I might content myself with replying that to
the scholarly mind anything is worthy of
study, if that study be thorough and system-
atic.   But I will go further, and say that at
the present time we need a far closer familiarity
with Sherlock's methods.   The evil that he
did lived after him, the good is interred with
him in the Reichenbach.   It is a known fact,
that is, that several people contracted the
dirty and deleterious habit of taking cocaine

as a result of reading the books. It is equally obvious that Scotland Yard has benefited not a whit either by his satire or by his example. When Holmes, in the *Mystery of the Red-Headed League*, discovered that certain criminals were burrowing their way into the cellars of a bank, he sat with a dark lantern in the cellar, and nabbed them quietly as they came through. But when the Houndsditch gang were found to be meditating an exactly similar design, what did the police authorities do? They sent a small detachment of constables, who battered on the door of the scene of operations at the bank, shouting, ' We think there is a burglary going on in here.' They were of course shot down, and the Home Office had to call out a whole regiment with guns and a fire brigade, in order to hunt down the survivors.

Any studies in Sherlock Holmes must be, first and foremost, studies in Dr. Watson. Let us treat at once of the literary and biblio-graphical aspect of the question. First, as to authenticity. There are several grave incon-sistencies in the Holmes cycle. For example the *Study in Scarlet* and the *Reminiscences* are from the hand of John H. Watson, M.D., but in the story of the *Man with the Twisted Lip*,

Mrs. Watson addresses her husband as James. The present writer, together with three brothers, wrote to ask Sir Arthur Conan Doyle for an explanation, appending their names in the proper style with crosses after them, and an indication that this was the sign of the Four. The answer was that it was an error, an error, in fact, of editing. ' Nihil aliud hic latet,' says the great Sauwosch, ' nisi redactor ignorantissi-mus.' Yet this error gave the original impetus to Backnecke's theory of the Deutero-Watson, to whom he assigns the *Study in Scarlet*, the *Gloria Scott*, and the *Return of Sherlock Holmes*. He leaves to the proto-Watson the rest of the Memoirs, the *Adventures*, the *Sign of Four* and the *Hound of the Baskervilles*. He disputed the *Study in Scarlet* on other grounds, the statement in it, for example, that Holmes's knowledge of literature and philosophy was nil, whereas it is clear that the true Holmes was a man of wide reading and deep thought. We shall deal with this in its proper place.

The *Gloria Scott* is condemned by Backnecke partly on the ground of the statement that Holmes was only up for two years at College, while he speaks in the *Musgrave Ritual* of ' my last years ' at the University ; which Backnecke supposes to prove that the two stories do not come from the same hand. The *Gloria Scott* further represents Percy Trevor's bull-dog as having bitten Holmes on his way down to Chapel, which is clearly untrue, since dogs are not allowed within the gates at either university. ' The bull-dog is more at home ' he adds ' on the Chapel steps, than this fraudulent imitation among the divine products of the Watsons-genius.' A further objection to the *Gloria Scott* is that it exhibits only four divisions out of the eleven-fold division (to be mentioned later) of the complete Holmes-episode, a lower percentage than is found in any other genuine story. For myself, however, I am content to believe that this irregularity is due merely to the exceptional character of the investigation, while the two inaccuracies are too slight (*me judice*) to form the basis for so elaborate a theory. I would include both the *Gloria Scott* and the *Study in Scarlet* as genuine incidents of Holmes-biography.

When we come to the *Final Problem*, the alleged death of Holmes, and his subsequent return in an unimpaired and even vigorous condition, the problem grows darker. Some critics, accepting the Return stories as genuine, regard the *Final Problem* as an incident faked by Watson for his own purposes; thus M. Piff-Pouff represents it as an old dodge of the thaumaturgist, and quotes the example of Salmoxis or Gebeleizis among the Getae, who hid underground for two years, and then returned to preach the doctrine of immortality. In fact, M. Piff-Pouff's verdict is thus expressed: 'Sherlockholmes has not at all fallen from the Reichenbach, it is Vatson who has fallen from the pinnacle of his mendacity.' In a similar vein, Bilgemann asserts that the episode is a weak imitation of Empedocles on Etna, the alpenstock being left behind to represent the famous slipper which was revomited by the volcano. 'The episode of the *Final Problem*' in his own immortal language, 'has the Watsons-applecart completely overturned.'

Others, Backnecke of course among them, regard the *Final Problem* as genuine, and the Return stories as a fabrication. The evidence against these stories may be divided into (a) those suggested by changes in the character and methods of Holmes, (b) those resting on impossibilities in the narrative itself, (c) inconsistencies found by comparison with the previous narrative.

(a) The true Holmes is never discourteous to a client: the Holmes of the *Adventure of the Three Students* 'shrugged his shoulders in ungracious acquiescence while our visitor . . . poured forth his story.' On the other hand, the true Holmes has no morbid craving for serious crime; but when John Hector Macfarlane talks of the probability of being arrested, the detective is represented as saying 'Arrest you! this is most grati—— most interesting.' Twice in the Return he gibes at his prisoner, a habit from which the true Holmes, whether from professional etiquette or for other reasons, invariably abstains. Again, the false Holmes actually calls a client by her Christian name, an impossible thing to an author whose views had not been distorted by the erroneous presentation of him in the play. He deliberately abstains from food while at work: the real Holmes only does so through absent-mindedness, as in the *Case of the Five Orange Pips*. He quotes Shakespeare in these stories alone, and that three times, without acknowledgement. He gives way to ludicrously bad logic in the *Dancing Men*. He sends Watson as his emissary in the *Solitary Cyclist*, and this is elsewhere unparalleled, for in the *Hound of the Baskervilles* he himself goes down to Dartmoor as well, to watch the case incognito. The true Holmes never splits an infinitive; the Holmes of the Return-stories splits at least three.

(b) Is it likely that a University scholarship paper—nay, an Oxford scholarship paper, for the Quadrangle is mentioned in connexion with it—should be printed only one day before the examination? That it should consist of only half a chapter of Thucydides? That this half-chapter should take the examiner an hour and a half to correct for the press? That the proofs of the half-chapter should be in three consecutive slips? Moreover, if a pencil was marked with the name JOHANN FABER, how could the two letters NN, and these two only, be left on the stump? Prof. J. A. Smith has further pointed out that it would be impossible to find out from the superimposition of the tracks of front and back bicycle tyres, whether the cyclist was going or coming.

(c) As to actual inconsistencies. In the mystery of the *Solitary Cyclist* a marriage is performed with no one present except the happy couple and the officiating clergyman. In the *Scandal in Bohemia* Holmes, disguised as a loafer, is deliberately called in to give away an unknown bride on the ground that the marriage will not be valid without a witness. In the *Final Problem*, the police secure ' the whole gang with the exception of Moriarty.' In the *Story of the Empty House* we hear that they failed to incriminate Colonel Moran. Professor Moriarty, in the Return, is called Professor James Moriarty, whereas we know from the *Final Problem* that James was really the name of his military brother, who survived him. And, worst of all, the dummy in the Baker Street window is draped in ' *the old mouse-coloured dressing-gown* '! As if we had forgotten that it was in a *blue* dressing-gown that Holmes smoked an ounce of shag tobacco at a sitting, while he unravelled the dark complication of the *Man with the Twisted Lip!* The detective, says M. Papier Maché, has become a chameleon. ' This is not the first time ' says the more ponderous Sauwosch, ' that a coat of many colours has been as a deception used! But in truth Sherlock, our modern Joseph, has altogether disappeared, and the evil beast Watson has him devoured.'

To this criticism I assent: I cannot assent, however, to the theory of the deutero-Watson. I believe that all the stories were written by

Watson, but whereas the genuine cycle actually happened, the spurious adventures are the lucubrations of his own unaided invention. Surely we may reconstruct the facts thus. Watson has been a bit of a gad-about. He is a spendthrift: so much we know from the beginning of the *Study in Scarlet*. His brother, as Holmes finds out by examining the scratches on the keyhole of his watch, was a confirmed drunkard. He himself, as a bachelor, haunts the Criterion Bar: in the *Sign of Four* he admits having had too much Beaune for lunch, behaves strangely at lunch, speaks of firing off a double-barrelled tiger-cub at a musket, and cautions his future wife against taking more than two drops of castor-oil, while recommending strychnine in large doses as a sedative. What happens? His Elijah is taken away from him: his wife, as we know, dies: he slips back into the grip of his old enemy; his practice, already diminished by continued neglect, vanishes away; he is forced to earn a livelihood by patching together clumsy travesties of the wonderful incidents of which he was once the faithful recorder.

Sauwosch has even worked out an elaborate table of his debts to other authors, and to the earlier stories. Holmes's stay in Thibet with the Grand Lama is due to Dr. Nikola: the cipher of the *Dancing Men* is read in the same manner as that in the *Gold Bug*, by Edgar Allan Poe: the *Adventure of Charles Augustus Milverton* shows the influence of Raffles. The *Norwood Builder* owes much to the *Scandal in Bohemia:* the *Solitary Cyclist* has the plot of the *Greek Interpreter:* the *Six Napoleons* of the *Blue Carbuncle:* the *Adventure of the Second Stain* is a doublet of the *Naval Treaty*, and so on.

We now pass on to the dating of the various pieces, so far as it can be determined by internal evidence, implicit or explicit. The results may be tabulated thus :

(1) The *Gloria Scott*—Holmes's first case.

(2) The *Musgrave Ritual*—his second.

(3) The *Study in Scarlet*—Watson first appears, i.e. the first of the We-Stories. Date 1879.

(4) 1883, the *Speckled Band*.

(5) 1887, April, the *Reigate Squires*.

(6) Same year, the *Five Orange Pips*.

(7) 1888, the *Sign of Four*—Watson becomes engaged.

(8) The *Noble Bachelor*. Then comes Watson's marriage, followed closely by

    (9) The *Crooked Man.*

    (10) The *Scandal in Bohemia*, and

    (11) The *Naval Treaty*, apparently in that order.

To some period in the year '88 we must assign 12, 13, and 14, that is, the *Stockbroker's Clerk*, the *Case of Identity*, and the *Red-Headed League*. In the June of '89 we have (15) the *Man with the Twisted Lip*, (16) the *Engineer's Thumb* (Summer), and (17) the *Blue Carbuncle* (somewhere in the octave of Christmas). The *Final Problem* is dated '91. Of the remainder, *Silver Blaze*, the *Yellow Face*, the *Resident Patient*, the *Greek Interpreter*, the *Beryl Coronet*, and the *Copper Beeches* are apparently before Watson's marriage, the *Boscombe Valley Mystery* after it: otherwise they are undated.

    There remains only the *Hound of the Baskervilles*. This is explicitly dated 1889, that is, it does not pretend to be after the Return. Sauwosch, who believes it to be spurious, points out that the *Times* would never have had a leader on Free Trade till after 1903. But this argument from internal evidence defeats itself: we can show by a method somewhat akin to that of Blunt's *Undesigned Coincidences in Holy Scriptures* that it was meant to be before

1901. The old crank who wants to have a law-suit against the police says it will be known as the case of Frankland versus REGINA—King Edward, as we all know, succeeded in 1901.

I must not waste time over other evidences (very unsatisfactory) which have been adduced to show the spuriousness of the *Hound of the Baskervilles*. Holmes's 'cat-like love of personal cleanliness' is not really inconsistent with the statement in the *Study in Scarlet* that he had pinpricks all over his hand covered with plaster —though this is also used by Backnecke to tell against the genuineness of the earlier production. A more serious question is that of Watson's breakfast-hour. Both in the *Study in Scarlet* and in the *Adventures* we hear that Watson breakfasted after Holmes: in the *Hound* we are told that Holmes breakfasted late. But then, the true inference from this is that Watson breakfasted very late indeed.

Taking, then, as the basis of our study, the three long stories, *Sign of Four*, *Study in Scarlet*, and *Hound of the Baskervilles*, together with the twenty-three short stories, twelve in the *Adventures*, and eleven in the *Memoirs*, we may proceed to examine the construction and the literary antecedents of this form of art. The actual scheme of each should consist, according to the German scholar, Ratzegger, followed by most of his successors, of eleven distinct parts; the order of them may in some cases be changed about, and more or less of them may appear as the story is closer to or further from the ideal type. Only the *Study in Scarlet* exhibits all the eleven; the *Sign of Four* and *Silver Blaze* have ten, the *Boscombe Valley Mystery* and the *Beryl Coronet* nine, the *Hound of the Baskervilles*, the *Speckled Band*, the *Reigate Squires*, and the *Naval Treaty* eight, and so on till we reach the *Five Orange Pips*, the *Crooked Man*, and the *Final Problem* with five, and the *Gloria Scott* with only four.

The first part is the Prooimion, a homely Baker Street scene, with invaluable personal touches, and sometimes a demonstration by the detective. Then follows the first explanation, or Exegesis kata ton diokonta, that is, the client's statement of the case, followed by the Ichneusis, or personal investigation, often including the famous floor-walk on hands and knees. No. 1 is invariable, Nos. 2 and 3 almost always present. Nos. 4, 5 and 6 are less necessary: they include the Anaskeue, or refutation on its own merits of the official theory of Scotland Yard, the first Promenusis (exoterike) which gives a few stray hints to the police, which they never adopt, and the second Promenusis (esoterike), which adumbrates the true course of the investigation to Watson alone. This is sometimes wrong, as in the *Yellow Face*. No. 7 is the Exetasis, or further following up of the trial, including the cross-questioning of relatives, dependants, etc., of the corpse (if there is one), visits to the Record Office, and various investigations in an assumed character. No. 8 is the Anagnorisis, in which the criminal is caught or exposed, No. 9 the second Exegesis (kata ton pheugonta), that is to say the criminal's confession, No. 10 the Metamenusis, in which Holmes describes what his clues were and how he followed them, and No. 11 the Epilogos, sometimes comprised in a single sentence. This conclusion is, like the Prooimion, invariable, and often contains a gnome or quotation from some standard author.

Although the *Study in Scarlet* is in a certain sense the type and ideal of a Holmes story, it is also to some extent a primitive type, of which elements were later discarded. The Exegesis kata ton pheugonta is told for the most part, not in the words of the criminal, but as a separate story in the mouth of the narrator : it also occupies a disproportionate amount of the total space. This shows directly the influence of Gaboriau : his *Detective's Dilemma* is one volume, containing an account of the tracing of the crime back to its author, who is of course a duke : the second volume, the *Detective's Triumph*, is almost entirely a retailing of the duke's family history, dating back to the Revolution, and we only rejoin Lecoq, the detective, in the last chapter. Of course, this method of telling the story was found long and cumbrous, but the French school has not yet seen through it, since the *Mystery of the Yellow Room* leaves a whole unexplained problem to provide copy for *The Perfume of the Lady in Black*.

But the literary affinities of Dr. Watson's masterly style are to be looked for further afield than Gaboriau, or Poe, or Wilkie Collins. M. Piff-Pouff especially, in his *Psychologie de Vatson*, has instituted some very remarkable parallels with the *Dialogues of Plato*, and with the Greek drama. He reminds us of the blustering manner of Thrasymachus when he first breaks into the argument of the Republic, and compares the entry of Athelney Jones : ' Oh, come, now, come ! Never be ashamed to own up ! But what's all this ? Bad business, bad business !

Stern facts here, no room for theories,' and so on. And when the detective comes back crest-fallen after a few days, wiping his brow with a red handkerchief, we remember how Socrates describes the first time in his life when he ever saw Thrasymachus blushing. The rival theories of Gregson and Lestrade only serve to illustrate the multiformity of error.

But the most important point is the nature of the Scotland Yard criticism. Lecoq has his rival, but the rival is his own superior in the detective force, thwarts his schemes out of pique, and actually connives at the prisoner's receiving notes through the window of his cell. The jealousy of a Lestrade has none of this paltry spirit about it, it is a combination of intellectual pride and professional pique. It is the opposition of the regular force to the amateur. Socrates was hated by the sophists because they took money, and he did not. The cases in which Holmes takes money, explicitly at any rate, are few. In the *Scandal in Bohemia* he is given £1,000, but this would seem to be only for current expenses, and may well have been refunded. At the end, he refuses the gift of an emerald ring. He will not allow the City and Suburban Bank to do more than pay his expenses in connection with the Red-headed League. He says the same elsewhere: ' As for my reward, my profession is my reward.' On the other hand, he takes £4,000 from Mr. Holder when he has recovered the missing beryls for £3,000. In the *Study in Scarlet*, when setting out in business, he says: ' I listen to their story, they listen to my comments, and then I pocket my fee.' In the *Greek Interpreter* he affirms that detection is a means of livelihood with him. And in the *Final Problem* we hear that he has been so well paid for his services in several instances to crowned heads that he is thinking of retiring from business and taking to chemistry. We must suppose, therefore, that he did sometimes take payment, but perhaps only where his clients could well afford it. None the less, as compared with the officials, he is a free lance: he has no axe to grind, no promotion to seek. And further, there is an antithesis of method. Holmes is determined not to be led away by side issues and apparent pressure of facts: this it is that raises him above the level of the sophists.

If the sophists have been borrowed from the Platonic dialogue, one element at least has been borrowed from the Greek drama. Gaboriau has no Watson. The confidant of Lecoq is an old soldier, preternaturally stupid, inconceivably inefficient. Watson provides what the Holmes drama needs—a Chorus. He represents the solid, orthodox, respectable view of the world in general; his drabness is accentuated by contrast with the limelight which beats upon the central figure. He remains stable amid the eddy and flux of circumstance.

> Ille bonis faveatque, et consilietur amicis,
> Et regat iratos, et amet peccare timentes:
> Ille dapes laudet mensae brevis, ille salubrem
> Justitiam, legesque, et apertis otia portis.
> Ille tegat commissa, deosque precetur et oret
> Ut redeat miseris, abeat fortuna superbis.

It is to Professor Sabaglione that we owe the profoundest study of Watson in this his choric character. He compares such passages as that in the *Speckled Band:*

Holmes: ' The lady could not move her bed. It must always be in the same relative position to the ventilator and the rope—for such we may call it, since it was clearly never meant for a bell-pull.'

Watson: ' Holmes, I seem to see what you are hinting at. We are only just in time to prevent some subtle and horrible crime.'

with the well-known passage in the Agamem-
non,

Cassandra: ' Ah, ah, keep away the bull
from the cow ! She takes him, the black-horned
one, in a net by her device, and smites him ; he
falls in a watery vessel—I speak to thee of the
Mystery of the Treacherous Cauldron.'

Chorus: ' Far be it from me to boast of any
particular skill in oracles, but I deduce from
these words some impending evil.'

Watson, like the Chorus, is ever in touch
with the main action, and seems to share the
full privileges of the audience ; yet, like the
Chorus, he is always about three stages behind
the audience in the unravelling of the plot.

And the seal, and symbol, and secret of
Watson is, of course, his bowler. It is not like
other bowlers : it is a priestly vestment, an
insigne of office. Holmes may wear a squash
hat, but Watson cleaves to his bowler, even at
midnight in the silence of Dartmoor, or on the
solitary slopes of the Reichenbach. He wears
it constantly, even as the archimandrite or the
rabbi wears his hat : to remove it would be
akin to the shearing of Samson's locks by
Delilah. ' Watson and his bowler ' says M. Piff-
Pouff, ' they are separable only in thought.' It

is his apex of wool, his petasus of invisibility, his *mitra pretiosa*, his triple tiara, his halo. The bowler stands for all that is immutable and irrefragable, for law and justice, for the established order of things, for the rights of humanity, for the triumph of the man over the brute. It towers colossal over sordidness and misery and crime : it shames and heals and hallows. The curve of its brim is the curve of perfect symmetry, the rotundity of its crown is the rotundity of the world. 'From the hats of Holmes's clients,' writes Professor Sabaglione, ' deduce themselves the traits, the habits, the idiosyncrasies : from the hat of Guatson deduces itself his character.' Watson is everything to Holmes—his medical adviser, his foil, his philosopher, his confidant, his sympathizer, his biographer, his domestic chaplain, but above all things else he stands exalted in history as the wearer of the unconquerable bowler hat.

And if the rival detectives are the sophists, and Watson is the Chorus, what of the clients, and what of the criminals? It is most important to remember that these are only secondary figures. 'The murderers of the Holmes cycle,' M. Papier Maché assures us, ' are of no more importance than the murderers are not in

Macbeth.' Holmes himself often deprecates
Watson's habit of making the stories too sensational, but he does him an injustice. The
authors of crime are not, in Watson, of personal
interest, like the Duke in Gaboriau; they have
no relation to the detective other than that
which subsists between the sleuth-hound and
its quarry—the author of the *Mystery of the
Yellow Room* was a bungler when he made
Jacques Rouletabille the criminal's natural son
—they are not animated by lofty or religious
motives like the high-flown villains in Mr.
Chesterton's *Innocence of Father Brown*. All clients
are model clients: they state their case in
flawless journalese; all criminals are model
criminals: they do the cleverest thing a criminal
could possibly do in the given circumstances.
By a sort of Socratic paradox, we might say that
the best detective can only catch the best thief.
A single blunder on the part of the guilty man
would have thrown all Holmes's deductions
out of joint. Love and money are their only
incentives: brutality and cunning their indefeas-
ible qualities.

And thus we arrive at the central figure
himself, and must try to gather together a few
threads in the complex and many-sided character.

There is an irony in the process, for Holmes liked to look upon himself as a machine, an inhuman and undifferentiated sleuth-hound. ' L'homme, c'est rien ; l'œuvre, c'est tout,' was one of his favourite quotations.

Sherlock Holmes was descended from a long line of country squires : his grandmother was the sister of a French artist : his elder brother Mycroft was, as we all know, more gifted than himself, but found an occupation, if the Reminiscences are to be trusted, in a confidential audit of Government accounts. Of Sherlock's school career we know nothing ; Watson was at school, and one of his schoolmates was the nephew of a peer, but this seems to have been exceptional there, since it was considered good fun to ' chevy him about the playground and hit him over the shins with a wicket.' This seems to dispose of the idea that Watson was an Etonian. On the other hand, we have no evidence as to his University career, except the testimony (always doubtful) of one of the Return stories that he was unacquainted with the scenery of Cambridgeshire. Of Holmes's student days our knowledge is much fuller : he was reserved by nature, and his recreations—boxing and fencing—did not make him many acquaintances.

One of his friends was Percy Trevor, son of an ex-convict, who had made his money in the Australian goldfields; another Reginald Musgrave, whose ancestors went back to the Conquest—quite the last word in aristocracy. He lived in a College, but what College? And at which University? The argument that his scientific bent would have naturally taken him to Cambridge defeats itself: for why should he have been only up two years if he wanted a proper scientific training? More and more as I consider the wealth of his two friends, the exclusive aristocracy of the one, and the doggy tendencies of the other, together with the isolation which put even so brilliant a light as Holmes's under a bushel—more and more I incline to the opinion that he was up at the House. But we have no sure evidence.

If he was an Oxford man, he was not a Greats' man. Yet when Watson describes his first impressions of the man at the beginning of the *Study in Scarlet*—the *locus classicus* for Holmes's characteristics—he wrongs him in saying that his knowledge of philosophy is nil, and his knowledge of literature nil. The fact is, clearly, that Holmes did not let his talents appear till he had been living with Watson for some time, and had come to recognize his sterling qualities. In fact, he compares Hafiz with Horace, quotes Tacitus, Jean Paul, Flaubert, Goethe, and Thoreau, and reads Petrarch in a G.W.R. carriage. He has no definite interest in philosophy as such, yet he holds certain definite views on scientific method. A philosopher could not have said, 'when you have eliminated the impossible, whatever remains, however improbable, must be the truth.' He could not have confused observation with inference, as Holmes does when he says: 'Observation shows me you have been to the Post Office' judging by the mud on Watson's boots. There must be inference here, though it may be called implicit inference, however rapid be the transition of thought. Yet Holmes was no Sensationalist. What sublimer confession of faith could any realist make than the remark in the *Study in Scarlet:* 'I ought to know by this time that when a fact appears to be opposed to a long train of deductions, it invariably proves to be capable of bearing some other interpretation'?

And here I must say a word on the so-called 'method of deduction.' M. Papier Maché has boldly asserted that it was stolen from Gaboriau. M. Piff-Pouff in his well-known article,

'Qu'est-ce que c'est que la déduction?' declares roundly that Holmes's methods were inductive. The two fallacies rest on a common ground. Lecoq has observation : he notices footsteps on the snow. He has powers of inference, for he can infer from such footsteps the behaviour of those who have left them. He has not the method of deduction—he never sits down and reasons out what it is probable the man would have done next. Lecoq has his lens and his forceps : he has not the dressing-gown and the pipe. That is why he has to depend on mere chance, again and again, for picking up lost threads. Holmes no more depended on a chance than he prayed for a miracle. That is why Lecoq, baffled after a long investigation, has to have recourse to a sort of arm-chair detective, who, without leaving the arm-chair, tells him exactly what must have happened. It is wrong to call this latter character, as M. Papier Maché does, the original of Mycroft : he is the original, if you will, of Sherlock. Lecoq is but the Stanley Hopkins, almost the Lestrade, of his period. Holmes himself has explained for us the difference between observation (or inference) and deduction. It is by observation *a posteriori* that he recognizes Watson's visit to the Post Office from the mud on his trousers; it is by deduction *a priori* that he knows he has been sending a telegram, since he has seen plenty of stamps and postcards in Watson's desk.

Let us now take two pictures of Sherlock Holmes, the one at leisure, the other at work. Leisure was, of course, abhorrent to him— more so than to Watson. Watson says he was reckoned fleet of foot, but we have only his own word for it, and Holmes always beat him; beyond this alleged prowess we have no evidence of Watson's athleticism, except that he could throw a rocket through a first-floor window. But Holmes had been a boxer and a fencer; during periods of enforced inactivity he fired a revolver at the opposite wall till he had 'marked it with the patriotic device V.R.' Violin playing occupied leisure moments when Watson first knew him, but later it seems to be nothing more than a relaxation after hard work. And —this is very important—in this music was the exact antithesis of cocaine. We never hear of the drug being used in order to stimulate the mental faculties for hard work. All the stimulus needed he derived from tobacco. We all know, of course, that he smoked shag; few people could say off-hand what his pipe was made of.

As a matter of fact, his tastes were various.
The long vigil in Neville St. Clair's house was
solaced by a briar—this is when he is hard at
work; when he sees his way through a problem
by inspection, as in the *Case of Identity*, he takes
down 'the old and oily clay pipe, which was to
him as a counsellor.'   In the *Copper Beeches* he takes
down ' the long cherrywood pipe with which he
was wont to replace his clay when he was in a
disputatious rather than a meditative mood.'
On one occasion he offers Watson snuff. Watson,
by the way, smoked Ship's tobacco when he
went into lodgings with Holmes, but must have
replaced it soon after with a sterner stuff, thinly
veiled under the *nom de plume* of Arcadia Mix-
ture. This expensive product he did not
abandon even under the exigencies of married
life; though his circumstances were not those
of affluence, since he had linoleum laid down
in the front hall.   But the pipe is not to Watson
what it is to Holmes: to Holmes belongs the
immortal phrase: ' This will be a three-pipe
problem.'   He is one of the world's great
smokers.

Now let us see Holmes at work. We all
know how brisk he becomes at the appearance
of a client; how, according to the inimitable

phrase in the Reminiscences: ' Holmes sat up
in his chair and took his pipe out of his mouth
like a hound that has heard the View Halloo.'
We have seen him in the mind's eye prowling
round the room with his nose an inch from the
ground, on the look-out for cigarette-ends,
orange-peel, false teeth, domes of silence, and
what not, that may have been left behind by
the criminal.   ' It is not a man,' says M. Binsk,
the great Polish critic, ' it is either a beast or a
god.'

It is this charge of inhumanity brought against
Holmes that I wish specially to rebut.   True,
he is reported to have been found beating the
dead subjects in the laboratory, to see whether
or no bruises could be produced after death.
True, he was a scientist.   True, we get passages
like that in the *Sign of Four:*

" Miss Morstan: From that day to this no
word has been heard of my unfortunate father.
He came home with his heart full of hope, to
find some peace, some comfort, and instead——

She put her hand to her throat, and a choking
sob cut short her utterance.   ' The date? '
asked Holmes, opening his notebook."

But is it true to say that Holmes's anxiety to
catch the criminal was not, like Watson's, due

to a passion for justice, but to a purely scientific interest in deduction? Such truths are never more than half-truths : it would be hard to say that the footballer plays only for the goal, or that he plays only for the sake of exercise. Humanity and science in Holmes are strangely blended. At one moment we find him saying ' Women are never to be trusted, not even the best of them' (the coward !) or asserting that he cannot agree with those who rank modesty among the virtues, since the logician must see all things exactly as they are. Even his little sermon on the rose in the *Naval Treaty* is delivered in order to cover the fact that he is examining the window-frame for scratches. At another moment he is purchasing ' something a little choice in white wines,' and discoursing on miracle plays, on Stradivarius violins, on the Buddhism of Ceylon, and on the warships of the future.

But there are two specially human characteristics which come out at the very moment of action. One is a taste for theatrical arrangement, as when he sends back five orange pips to the murderers of John Openshaw, or takes a sponge into prison with which to unmask the man with the Twisted lip, or serves up the

Naval Treaty under a cover as a breakfast dish. The other is a taste for epigram. When he gets a letter from a duke, he says: ' It looks like one of those social summonses which call upon a man either to be bored or to lie.' There is a special kind of epigram, known as the Sherlockismus, of which the indefatigable Ratzegger has collected no less than one hundred and seventy-three instances. The following may serve as examples:

' Let me call your attention to the curious incident of the dog in the night-time.'

' The dog did nothing at all in the night-time.'

' That was the curious incident,' said Sherlock Holmes :—

and again :

' I was following you, of course.'

' Following me? I saw nobody.'

' That is what you must expect to see when I am following you,' said Sherlock Holmes.

To write fully on this subject would need two terms' lectures at least. Some time, when leisure and enterprise allow, I hope to deliver them. Meanwhile, I have thrown out these hints, drawn these outlines of a possible mode of treatment. You know my methods, Watson: apply them.

VI

A RAMBLE
IN
BARSETSHIRE

VI

A RAMBLE IN BARSETSHIRE

(In the footnotes the following abbreviations are used:
" B.T." for *Barchester Towers*, " F.P." for *Framley Parsonage*,
" S.H." for *The Small House at Allington*, " L.C." for *The Last
Chronicle of Barset*.)

" To me Barset has been a real county,
and its city a real city, and the spires
and towers have been before my eyes, and the
voices of the people are known to my ears, and
the pavements of the city ways are familiar
to my footsteps." Trollope's boast, or confession,
can be echoed by most of his modern readers :
Barsetshire lives chiefly as a cult, and the profane
seldom violate the Cathedral precincts, or flutter
the rooks that cawed answer to the Archdeacon's
" Good Heavens ! " after his first call on the
Proudies. For the initiated, Barchester has
reality, and how different a thing is reality in
literature from realism ! Only a few isolated
figures in letters stand out as real : Sir Roger
de Coverley, I suppose, Mr. Pickwick certainly,

and of course Sherlock Holmes, who should
have had his statue erected in Baker Street
before ever Kensington Gardens were dedicated
to Peter Pan: most of us could name a dozen,
chosen with a certain amount of individual
caprice, but hardly more, of such characters.
Such characters, I mean, as create a real
illusion; so that a man attaining Heaven might
look round him and say, " And now, where's
Pickwick? Oh, no, I forgot; of course he's
only a character in a book! "

Whether Trollope be held to have created
such individual figures or no, it is certain that
he has added one to the list of English counties.
Externally, the trick depends merely on the
continued handling of a single set of puppets,
who achieve immortality by mere force of not
disappearing in the last chapter. Married they
may be, but we know we shall have glimpses
later of their married happiness; though they
remain unwed, there are still brides to be wooed
in the next volume—prebends, too, waiting for
the black-coated ones. Only Mr. Harding is
resolute in his refusal of the purple, as Lily Dale
of the orange-blossom—though, indeed, Lily
Dale is not a Barsetshire character: Guestwick
and Allington were over the county border,

and it is no disloyalty to the genius of the
county to admit (as many readers would have
to admit) that Lily Dale bores you. And not
only the characters, but the places, the distances,
the dating of the history remain constant
factors from one volume to the next, so that
until Mr. Crawley's new coat is installed at
St. Ewold's there is no such word as farewell.

Distances and dates are, above all things,
treacherous ground for the novelist, so that
most authors deal with them in dubious allusions,
fearful of being caught out later : enough for
their ambition of consistency if they can keep
the heroine's hair uniform in colour through
four hundred pages. Trollope is bolder than
this ; he is profuse of detail, trusting either to a
methodical mind to ensure consistency, or to his
very audacity to bluff his readers. Which is it,
really? It is commonly said by his admirers
that he never trips ; that is nonsense ; he is not
even certain whether the inn whose freehold
Mrs. Bold inherited was *The Dragon of Wantly*
or a mere *George and Dragon*. But there is enough
consistency, on the face of it, to tempt a pedant
to the detailed examination of the whole subject.
How far can Barsetshire be reconstructed?
How far its history?

The map should always come first, as the diagram in Euclid. In drawing it I have been forced to assume that the roads were, roughly speaking, straight ones : Barchester was the old Baronum Castrum, and we should expect some trace of our first civilizers : zigzag routes might, here and there, help us out of a difficulty, but it is a help we have no right to assume. Once, in *Framley Parsonage*, Trollope doubts whether he had not better provide his public with a map ; if he had yielded to that inspiration, here is what I think he would have had to draw :

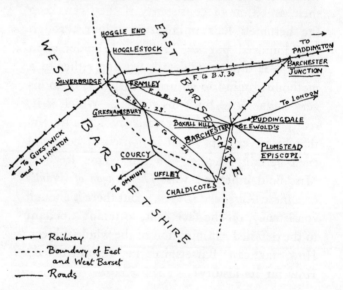

For the geography of Barsetshire we have two clear landmarks, the railway and the division of the county into East and West. Barchester itself is in the West of England, and the London line, therefore, approaches it from the East. It stands off the main line, connected with a station called (presumably) Barchester Junction, of some dignity, for it had a refreshment-room (though Dr. Thorne would not call the tea there tea).[1] And the branch was of some importance; three trains ran each way, to the scandal of Mrs. Proudie, on the Sabbath Day[2]—although five years earlier, when Mr. Harding bolted up to London unknown to the Archdeacon, the week-day service was a thin one, and no train could discharge those formidable gaiters between the night-mail and the 2 p.m. at Paddington.[3] Silverbridge is the only other station named in the county, and this was clearly West of the Junction, for it was (as we shall see) over thirty miles distant from it, and stood close to the borders of East Barset. Courcy is also said to have had a station within a mile and a half of it, which had ruined the glories of its coaching days (Ch. 15 of *Dr. Thorne*), but this statement we shall prove to be false.

[1] *Dr. Thorne*, 46.   [2] B.T., 5.   [3] *The Warden*, 16.

In Ch. 14 of *Framley Parsonage*, the *locus classicus* of Barset geography, we are explicitly told that Hogglestock was a little north of the main line. Hoggle End was two miles to the North again[1]; with these exceptions, all the places we hear of are clearly South of it. Framley was close to the line, a little South of it; I cannot imagine why it had no station, unless this was due to the Conservative attitude of old Lady Lufton. Silverbridge was the station both for Framley (four miles) and for Hogglestock (six miles) : the distance between Framley and Hogglestock is uniformly reckoned at about seven miles ; we have thus a triangle, crossing the railway, which begins to fix our geographical data. Further, we know that Silverbridge (for which Plantagenet Palliser sat) was just in the Western division of the county, whereas Hogglestock and Framley and Greshamsbury (eight miles nearer Barchester) were in the Eastern and Conservative division. Chaldicotes, then, the home and the seat of poor Nat Sowerby, till the proceeds of the Oil of Lebanon reclaimed it for Dr. and Mrs. Thorne, will be to the South of Barchester, otherwise it could not be reckoned in West Barset. Chaldicotes, when Mark

[1] L.C., 12.

Robarts went there for his gravely suspected visit, was twenty-four miles from Framley.[1] And on that disastrous day, the morrow of Harold Smith's lecture, when Robarts went back to preach in aid of New Guinea missions, and was made late for the service through the overnight festivities of his Parliamentary friends, it was a ten-mile drive from Barchester.[2] How far, then, was Barchester from Framley? The subject is riddled with difficulties.

Framley stood a little off the Hogglestock-Barchester Road, so that Mr. Toogood readily consented to let Major Grantly call at the Vicarage to see Grace Crawley on his way back to the city.[3] The point of junction is Framley Mill, where Farmer Mangle put down Mr. Crawley on that adventurous journey to the Palace which ended in his telling Mrs. Proudie to stick to her distaff.[4] On the same occasion it is definitely stated that the distance from Barchester to Hogglestock was one of fifteen miles. I suppose it was on the same reckoning that Mr. Thumble, coming over to arrange about taking Sunday duty, achieved the distance in something over two hours, though the Bishop's cob was only accustomed to a twelve-

[1] F.P., 3.   [2] *Ibidem.*   [3] L.C., 74.   [4] L.C., 17.

mile radius from the Palace, and he broke its knees on Spigglewick Hill.[1] But this is clearly a false calculation, for it would make Framley itself only nine miles from the Cathedral city. A more generous estimate makes Dean Arabin undertake a journey of forty miles to Hogglestock and back when he goes over to see Mrs. Crawley in her illness[2]; that will give us thirteen miles between Barchester and Framley. The *Last Chronicle* itself seems to agree with such an estimate when it puts Silverbridge twenty miles from Barchester by road (though even that would be an over-statement).[3]

But even this will not do. Framley is twenty-four miles as the crow flies from Chaldicotes; Chaldicotes is ten miles from Barchester; how could even Professor Einstein persuade us that the third side of the triangle was only thirteen miles long? We are forced to conclude that the real distance was twenty miles from Framley to Barchester, and that our author has accident-ally made this the distance from Hogglestock to Barchester. He doubles the mistake when he gives Henry Grantly a ride of twenty miles from Plumstead) which lay the other side of Barchester)

[1] L.C., 63.   [2] F.P., 36.
[3] L.C., ch. 11 (20 by road, more than 40 by rail).

to inform the Crawleys at Hogglestock that all is well about the cheque; it was really a drive of thirty-two miles that the Archdeacon's horses were allowed to take on this unique occasion.[1]

An alternative route between Barchester and Silverbridge, the railway centre for West Barset, lay through Boxall Hill, the home of the Scatcherds (seven and a half miles), Greshamsbury (another seven and a half miles), and eight miles beyond that (twenty-three miles in all). Silverbridge was the post-town for Greshamsbury, and I cannot make out why it was not the station rather than Barchester on its branch, unless Silverbridge was neglected by the fast trains. West of Silverbridge the railway takes you to Guestwick, in a neighbouring county, which was the station for Allington: it was from Allington that Johnny Eames was returning when Adolphus Crosbie, fresh from the glories of Courcy Castle, boarded his carriage at Barchester Junction, all unwitting of the black eye that awaited him at Paddington.[2] Where, then, was Courcy? According to Ch. 15 of *Dr. Thorne* it lay within a mile and a half of the railway. But, if so, how is it that the Courcy mail passed by road through Uffley

[1] L.C., 73.   [2] S.H., 34.

and Chaldicotes (where it picked up Mark Robart's letter to his wife) to Barchester, and so by rail to Barchester Junction, and back from there to Silverbridge and Framley?[1] Even the G.P.O. could hardly be responsible for such an arrangement. How, again, could Adolphus Crosbie, even though he had time to waste, come all the way round by the Junction and Barchester, and take a carriage on, in order to reach Courcy from Allington?[2] Courcy was certainly in the Western division; and according to the *Small House* it was twelve miles from Silverbridge. We must not put it too far from Barchester, or, again, the thrifty Adolphus would have used Silverbridge as his station : he would have missed his chance interview with Mr. Harding, but I think Dr. Tempest would have offered him biscuits and wine, as he did to Mr. Crawley. It must be well to the South, or the course of its mail through Chaldicotes becomes impossibly circuitous. I have, therefore, put it some twelve miles from Barchester, the direction West with a little South in it. Omnium was within an after-dinner drive of Courcy (and the epithet may perhaps be strongly stressed, in view of the Honourable

[1] F.P., 5.   [2] S.H., 16.

George's condition) : more than six miles away, for Frank Gresham had walked that distance before the gig overtook him.[1]

Puddingdale is only four miles from Barchester, and its direction ought to be Eastwards, for Mrs. Quiverful is put down by Farmer Subsoil at the bridge when she goes to invoke Mrs. Proudie in her behalf[2]—the river flowed close to Hiram's Hospital, which adjoined the London Road and the Cathedral Close.[3] The London Road must have been on the East, and the statement on the very first page of *The Warden* that the Cathedral was at the West End of the town is an error—Trollope did not know then how vast a fabric he was beginning to erect. When, at last made a happy woman, she is moving her belongings into the hospital, the Archdeacon passes her on his way back to Plumstead Episcopi, and raises his hat to her in his triumph over the Deanery[4] : this means that the Plumstead road also entered Barchester from the East. I suspect that Puddingdale lay on the London Road, and the way to Plumstead branched off from it earlier. Plumstead should, if anything, be put South of the road, since there is never any question of travelling from it to Framley except through the city.

[1] *Dr. Thorne*, 19.   [2] B.T., 25.   [3] *The Warden*, 1.   [4] B.T., 50.

How far was Plumstead from Barchester?
The distance there and back was under ten
miles in the *Last Chronicle* ; yet Dr. Fillgrave was
five or six miles from home, at Plumstead,
when Sir Roger Scatcherd sent for him.[1]   Meanwhile, in *Barchester Towers* the distance one way
is reckoned at nine miles.   The discrepancy
cannot be explained away ; perhaps it is simplest
to take the middle estimate.   St. Ewold's lies
off the road to Plumstead, at a distance of only
one mile from the city ; so that it cannot really
have taken the Archdeacon and Mr. Harding
three miles out of their way when they went
to congratulate Arabin on his elevation to the
Deanery.[2]   Ullathorne is clearly in the village
of St. Ewold's : unless, then, the East Barset
roads were circuitous as well as muddy,
Countess de Courcy cannot really have started
at eleven and arrived at the Fête Champêtre
at three—probably the Honourable John was
nearer the truth in saying that they did not
start till one.[3]   Some puzzles remain unsolved.
Why did the Grantlys sleep at Framley when
they went over to dine, but not the Chaldicotes
Thornes, who had come almost the same
distance?[4]   Why did Caleb Oriel need to sleep

[1] *Dr. Thorne*, 12.   [2] B.T., 50.   [3] B.T., 37.   [4] L.C., 10.

at Framley when business took him to Silverbridge, only eight miles from home?[1]   And how
on earth did Mark Robarts go from Framley
to Silverbridge by railway?[2]   Though indeed
Major Grantly seems to have gone from Silverbridge to Guestwick viâ Paddington![3]   But
we must not press our author too much in
detail.

It will be seen that while Silverbridge,
Courcy, Omnium, and Chaldicotes were in
West Barset, and therefore in the Whig sphere
of influence, all the other places we know and
love were in the true-blue region—though we
are aware that old Mr. Gresham had his ter-
giversations.   There is, it will be observed, a
continual border warfare in progress.   Boxall
Hill fell into the power of the Radicals when
Sir Roger Scatcherd made Mr. Gresham part
with it; and I suspect it was during this period
that the suggestion was made of the Crown
buying up Chaldicotes Chase.   Just when it
seemed that Greshamsbury itself was to go the
way of Boxall Hill, Mary Thorne brought them
both back into the Gresham family and the
Tory camp.   If the Duke had succeeded in
buying up Chaldicotes from Nathaniel Sowerby,

[1] L.C., 54.   [2] L.C., 68.   [3] L.C., 27.

its Whig partisanship would have been guaranteed; instead, the Dunstable-Thorne alliance handed it over to the opposite camp, and (though I do not believe that Dr. Thorne ever went into politics) I have little doubt that Mr. Sowerby's successor was defeated before long. Barchester itself, in spite of its position, was always under Omnium influence, and its representation passed from Mr. Moffatt to Mr. Gazebee soon after that short interval when Sir Roger won it for the extreme left.

It will have been seen that, in his geographical detail, at any rate, Trollope is not the model of accuracy he has sometimes been thought. Other charges of forgetfulness may be laid against him. We may pass over some curious differences of spelling: Plumstead, for example, is Plumpstead in *Dr. Thorne*, and Archdeacon Grantly is Archdeacon Grantley; Mr. Gazebee appears as Mr. Gagebee in *Framley Parsonage*, and Dr. Fillgrave as Dr. Filgrave throughout the *Last Chronicle*. But is even the chronology accurate? It can, I think, be shown that, like the geography, it is consistent in its main skeleton, but has curious lapses in detail.

Letters in *The Warden* are dated simply " 18—" ; Mr. Harding at this time is nearly sixty years old,[1] Eleanor is twenty-four. In the *Last Chronicle*, where Mr. Harding is seventy-eight[2] and Eleanor is well over forty, letters are dated " 186—." *The Warden*, then, should be somewhere round 1850 ; *Barchester Towers* is explicitly five years later. Dr. Stanhope, the Signora Neroni's father, is recently dead in *Dr. Thorne*. The eponymous hero of that book, a bachelor to its last page, marries Miss Dunstable in *Framley Parsonage.* Letters in all these three books are dated " 185—." Letters in *The Small House* are dated " 186—" ; the status of Johnny Eames shows it to be earlier in date than the *Last Chronicle*. Can the dating be established with closer accuracy? In certain cases it can ; Frank Gresham came of age in 1854, and this fixes *Dr. Thorne*. Now, Dr. Thorne was six or seven years older than Squire Gresham,[3] who was twenty-four in 1834[4] ; Dr. Thorne, then, was born about 1804. This makes him fifty in the book that is named after him ; when he proposes to Miss Dunstable in *Framley Parsonage* he gives his age as fifty-five. In that book Mr. Crawley is forty and Grace Crawley nine ; in the *Last Chronicle* Mr. Crawley is fifty and Grace nine-

[1] *The Warden*, 1.   [2] L.C., 58.   [3] *Dr. Thorne*, 3.   [4] *Dr. Thorne*, 1.

teen. Thus *Dr. Thorne* should be 1854, *Framley
Parsonage* 1859, the *Last Chronicle* 1869. The five-
year interval between *The Warden* and *Barchester Towers* (which must be before 1854)
pushes back the date of *The Warden* at least
to 1849—let us call it 1848, which would make
Mr. Harding fifty-seven, just capable of being
described as "verging on sixty years." (It
may be observed, however, that in Ch. 14 of
Barchester Towers Mr. Harding is all but sixty-
five; he was meant, then, to be all but sixty
in *The Warden*.) In *The Small House* Lady
Dumbello, once Griselda Grantly (what years
ago it seems!) is said to have been two years
married. Thus the whole dating may be
approximately fixed: *The Warden*, '48; *Barchester Towers*, '53; *Dr. Thorne*, '54; *Framley
Parsonage*, '59; *The Small House at Allington*,
'61; the *Last Chronicle*, '69.

If this scheme is accurate, how can it be true
that Mrs. Proudie had been scarcely ten years
in Barchester at the time of her death?[1] By
our reckoning it was a full sixteen. She died
at the age of fifty-six, and was, therefore, only
forty when she came to Barchester; it is curious
that at that time her daughters were "all

[1] L.C., 67.

grown up and fit for fashionable life."[1] The Lady Amelia did not marry Mortimer Gazebee till four years after her excellent advice to Augusta Gresham as to marrying a commoner[2]; that is to say, she was engaged in 1859 at the earliest (for Frank Gresham's birthday is more than a year past by the end of *Dr. Thorne*), yet she is " the happy mother of many babies " in *The Small House* (1861).[3] Griselda Grantly is already seventeen in *Barchester Towers :* how comes it that in *Framley Parsonage*, when she ought to be twenty-three, she can be described as " little older " than Lucy Robarts, who is sixteen?[4] Henry Grantly was her elder brother, and in the *Last Chronicle* he is under thirty[5]; in *The Warden*, then, she should be less than nine, yet she has grown to be seventeen in the five years that have elapsed before *Barchester Towers*. Finally, Miss Dunstable is only thirty in *Dr. Thorne*, yet in *Framley Parsonage*, five years later, she is described as " well over forty."[6] Homer, it seems, has nodded.

Or, rather, Trollope has nodded : poor Homer would not be allowed, by our modern critics, nearly so much nodding-space. What blunder-

[1] B.T., 3.
[2] *Dr. Thorne*, 38.
[3] S.H., 17.
[4] F.P., 11.
[5] L.C., 2.
[6] F.P., 28.

ing redactors, what recensions, what insertions
of spurious lines, what contamination of documents would have been invoked if all these
inconsistencies were laid to the charge of the
ancient author! I will do it some day: the
most peccant redactor shall be the " Crawley-
inserter," a gentleman with an obvious *tendenz*,
since he is out for the redistribution of clerical
incomes, a project far from the ambitions of
the proto-Trollope. Hogglestock, of course, is
a mere " doublet " of Puddingdale; Mr.
Crawley's drive and walk to the Palace a
" doublet " of Mrs. Quiverful's drive and walk
to the Palace; the business of the cheque is
a sensational imitation of Mark Robarts' money
difficulties, Henry Grantly's infatuation a dupli-
cate of Lord Lufton's. The clumsy imitator
shall be blamed for want of originality, because
he didn't marry Johnny Eames to Lily Dale;
on the next page he shall be blamed for want
of sympathy with his original, because he dared
to kill Mrs. Proudie: I see it all. By the time
we have finished with the *Last Chronicle* I believe
Crosbie shall be its hero.

Consistency is, in romance, almost unattain-
able; if Homer missed it, so did Virgil, so did
Mallory, so did Spenser a hundred times:

there is even a mistake in the *Wrong Box*. Where
it obtrudes itself, suspect the hand of the con-
taminator : it is up to Arctinus to mind his
P's and Q's. Trollope certainly had, considering the quantity of his output and the fullness
of his detail, more consistency than is common
among authors of fiction ; to say that he was
sometimes inconsistent is to say no more than
that he was a man.

Is it only because they are so nearly men and
women that our eyelids quiver on the verge of
tears over the conventional tragedies of Trollope's characters? Or do we regret the passing
of something that was not mere shadow, a
world we were not born into, yet one that
coloured for us the outlook of boyhood, when
Archdeacons really preserved and drank port
and quoted Horace, and country doctors dared
to roll their own pills, and Lady Luftons
brooded like a visible Providence over the
country-side, and old Hiram's will, violated
though it might be in the letter, was better
kept in the spirit than our modern Quiverfuls
keep it, and clerical controversies, however
disedifying, did at least command the attention
of the whole reading public, not mere circles
of devotees? Here, surely, the optimist has

the advantage of the satirist. It is a cold triumph that we enjoy now over the Bumbles and the Stigginses that are so long dead; the vinegar has lost its bite with age, whether it be that of Dr. Pessimist Anticant or that of Mr. Popular Sentiment. But Trollope's rose-hued world, like a cloistral port (Dr. Middleton, surely, had held preferment in Barset), is all the better for keeping; Barchester, caught once for all by the artist's brush in a moment of mellow sunset, lives on, uncontaminated by change, in that attitude.

> Ah, happy, happy boughs, that cannot shed
>   Your leaves, nor ever bid the spring adieu!

Barchester, unlike its sister Sees, has been preserved from pushful clerico-journalists with their sermons on topics of the day, from the ravages of muscular Christianity, from Funds and Movements and Leagues and all the admirable but unsightly organizing tactics of our times, as surely as the lanes of Barsetshire have been saved from the motorist and its parks from a horde of degenerate Dunstables. There is no series of novels which more invite the continuator, none whose continuation would be more surely written down a sacrilege.

VII

THE IDENTITY
OF THE
PSEUDO-BUNYAN

VII

THE IDENTITY OF THE PSEUDO-BUNYAN.

THE PROGRESS of criticism, which has already had such gratifying effects in quickening the wits, dispelling the illusions, and consequently (it need hardly be said) strengthening the faith of the last two generations, may be compared to that of a young and voracious animal, whose appetite food whets but does not satiate, invigorating while it distends. Scarcely had the bones and sinews of Homer been separated, labelled, and hung out to dry, when the Old Testament was called into requisition, Moses being resolved into a whole syndicate of press-cutting agencies, and Isaiah multiplied into a goodly fellowship of prophets. Next it was the turn of Luke and Paul, the only New Testament authors who seemed genuine enough to be worth dismemberment. It is

hardly surprising, then, that in our own day
the *Pilgrim's Progress* should have gone the way
of the Bible, and that the authenticity of one
half or the other should be strenuously denied
by such conservative critics as are content to
admit the authenticity of either.

It is no part of our present purpose to discuss
the reasons which have been brought forward,
notably by Professor *Sack-the-Lot*, for refusing
altogether to a journeyman tinker the credit
for what he describes as " a work of finished
scholarship and profound theological acumen."
On the whole, it may be said that the pendulum
of criticism has swung back, and that a considerable number of scholars, both in England
and in Germany, are content to allow that at
least the majority of Part One came from the
hand of its reputed author. In the present
essay, I shall only recapitulate the considerations which, it is now recognized, make it
impossible to attribute Part Two to the same
writer, and then offer certain further suggestions
about the mystery which has hitherto shrouded
the identity of Christiana's biographer.

In setting out the proofs of dual authorship,
I shall hardly do more than restate the case
which has been put fully and finally in Canon

Wrest-the-Word's judicious monograph. The main contention rests upon:

(1) Inconsistencies in the narrative of Part Two as compared with Part One. These confront us, it is well known, at the very outset of the story. Christiana repeatedly bewails the fact that she refused to accompany her husband upon his pilgrimage, although he requested her to do so, e.g., on page 193 (the references given are to Pickering's edition of 1847 throughout). Whereas a glance at page 4 suffices to show that Christian, from the moment when he learned that he must go on a pilgrimage, ran away from home, shutting his ears to the protests of his family and not even attempting to answer them. It is true that the same careless error occurs on page 49, in the first half of the volume. But Mr. *Tithe-mint's* investigations have shown conclusively that this whole passage which refers to Piety, Charity and Prudence is a later interpolation in Part One. Again, Christian is unable to see the Wicket-gate from the City of Destruction, yet Christiana sees it without difficulty (pages 3, 196). The Wicket-gate is opened to Christian by " a grave person named Good-will " (page 20) ; whereas " the Keeper of the Gate " in Part Two is clearly treated as a

Divine Being (page 207). Christian, on page
20, is hastily pulled through the gate for fear
he should be wounded by an arrow from Beelze-
bub's Castle; Christiana and Mercy, on page
211, are in danger, not from long-distance fire,
but from a dog, which has never been mentioned in Part One at all.

It would be tedious to describe in detail all
the inconsistencies which occur in the body of
the work; suffice it to call attention to those
which are concerned with the final stages of the
pilgrimage. The Shepherds of the Delectable
Mountains are represented as having a Palace,
and there is a reference to Christian's slaying a
serpent, an incident which finds no place whatever in the genuine narrative. In the final
scene, where Christiana and her companions
pass over the river, no allusion is made to any
difficulty in negotiating the passage; the
imitator has apparently forgotten that in Part
One it was a matter of laborious effort to cross
the river without being swept off your feet,
and that Christian himself was very nearly
drowned in the middle of it. Finally, the scope
of the dream is unnecessarily restricted in Part
Two; Bunyan sees his pilgrims across the river
and safely into the city itself; the imitator, in

whom conscience has bred timorousness, loses sight of the characters before they cross.

(2) Hardly less confusion is observable if we trace carefully the time-scheme of the whole expedition, as it is represented in the two sections of the work. Christiana and the children pass their first night of travel at the Interpreter's house (page 228), and there is no sign that they have done less than a fair day's journey; their second night is similarly spent at the House Beautiful (page 247), and it is expressly stated that they reach it late at night (page 244). Whereas Christian makes a single day's journey of the whole distance to the House Beautiful (page 51), and even so, has only himself to thank for his benighted arrival—he has wasted time by leaving his roll on the Hill Difficulty, and having to go back for it (page 43). " Surely a large allowance," says Canon *Obvious*, in his happy way, " for the frailty of the weaker sex."[1] Conversely, it would appear that Christian spent his next night of travelling in the Valley of the Shadow, whereas the later pilgrims take refreshment after passing the end of the Valley, and reach the house of Gaius that same evening

[1] *Dear Old Bunyan*, p. 81. I owe much to Canon Obvious's book all through this essay.

(pages 65, 275, 290). The next stage takes either party to Vanity Fair. Christian and Faithful appear to reach the Fair in full daylight, or, at least, while trade is still brisk; Christiana and her companions have the start of them on this occasion, since they have lodged with Gaius; yet "it was eventide by that they got to the outside of the town" (page 307), and Mr. Mnason, their new host, tells them that they have "come a good stitch." From Vanity Fair to Doubting Castle is a day's march for both parties (pages 120, 318). From that point Christian and Hopeful reach the Land of Beulah without a night's pause, whereas Christiana takes two days over it, breaking her journey at the Delectable Mountains (pages 168, 321, 343).

The credit of having unmasked these inconsistencies is due to the invaluable work of Mr. *Muck-rake*, the pioneer in this field of criticism. But, as he himself points out, " these are surface inconsistencies compared with the root difficulty which underlies them all. The fact is, that whereas Christian goes on a pilgrimage, Christiana goes on a walking-tour."[1] Christian, he points out, only once voluntarily delays his

[1] *On the Trail of the Pilgrims*, Appendix II.

journey, and that only for a single day, at the House Beautiful. It is probably implied that he was for some time detained at Vanity Fair, and for three days he was immured in Doubting Castle (page 121). Apart from this, he is continually going forward, and husbanding his time like a man in a hurry; the whole action does not occupy, probably, more than a fortnight. In Part Two the sense of urgency has entirely disappeared. Christiana and her companions stop a whole month at the House Beautiful, and show no impatience to be on the march. Even longer intervals of time are postulated by the marrying and giving in marriage which complicates the rest of the book. Christiana's four sons are referred to repeatedly as " her sweet babes " at the beginning of the story. After the lapse, apparently, of a little over a month, the reader is confronted with a couple of weddings ! Strange enough that Matthew, who when last heard of was climbing over a garden wall to pick fruit " as boys are apt to do " (page 212), should now be old enough to marry Mercy ; it is even more astonishing that Phebe, Gaius' daughter, should give her hand to James, who was actually the youngest of the four (page 249). With Mr. Mnason at Vanity Fair the pilgrims stay " a

great while," and the two remaining sons are
duly paired off. Before they have reached the
Delectable Mountains, all four couples have
children, who are left behind at a kind of
orphanage provided for that purpose (page 316).
In a word, if Christian's pilgrimage took four-
teen days, it is difficult not to conclude that
Christiana's took as many years !

Mr. *Jettison Cargo* has recently attempted to
re-establish the author's credit by deleting all
these references to matrimony as spurious ; but
his account of the matter wears a pitiful air of
special pleading. The brute fact is that in Part
Two a wholly different conception of the allegory has been substituted. Bunyan fore-
shortened the whole of human life so as to make
it fit into the limits of a single journey. His
imitator provides us with a fully fledged
biography, and the pilgrimage-*motiv* has altogether fallen into the background.

(3) It seems incredible that, during all the
years in which the *Pilgrim's Progress* has been
thumbed by millions of readers, nobody should
have been struck by the enormous significance
of the metres employed in the incidental poetry,
until Canon *Wrest-the-Word* drew attention to it.
The genuine Bunyan always writes heroics. There

is not a single exception to this rule in the whole of Part One, although the author breaks into poetry on no less than twenty-nine occasions. In Part Two, the heroics are often doled out to us a couplet at a time, and even so, there are only eleven instances of their use. The author's favourite vehicle of expression in verse is " Common Metre," that is, alternate Iambic dimeters and Iambic tripodies, the latter rhymed—the system, in fact, of Auld Lang Syne. This scheme occurs no less than thirteen times, and there are instances of other metres on pages 263 and 333. It is well known that Canon *Wrest-the-Word* proceeded, on this ground, to attribute the authorship of Part Two to Nahum Tate, joint author of the Psalm-paraphrases and subsequently Poet Laureate. It is safe to say, however, that this attribution has now been abandoned by scholars. " The popularity of the Paraphrases," as Canon *Obvious* reminds us, " would naturally lead to widespread imitation."

(4) Canon *Wrest-the-Word* is perhaps inclined to attach too much importance to the argument from grammar. The work belongs, throughout, to a transition period in which " thou " and " you " are employed indifferently to express the second person singular. It is true that

whereas " thou " and its derivatives enjoy equal
popularity in both parts (52 : 53), " you " is
more frequent in Part One (81 usages against
64). Canon *Wrest-the-Word* insists strongly upon
the discrepancy ; he was trained in an exact
school, and for many years held the chair of
Dichotomy at Wolverhampton. But Canon
Obvious has pleaded, not without force, that
allowances must be made for mere coincidence.
On the other hand, it is at least worthy of note
that the curious syntactical usage " You was "
occurs three times in Part Two (pages 209, 247,
275), a licence quite unparalleled in Part One.

So far we have only been concerned to estab-
lish the spuriousness of Part Two ; and it is
difficult to see how men of Mr. *Jettison Cargo's*
undoubted scholarship and piety can still credit
its authenticity. If further proof were needed,
it has been contributed by a striking essay which
has recently come from the pen of Dr. *Cheese-
Paring*. " The age of cryptograms," he writes,
" which had begun with Bacon, had not yet
spent its force by the second half of the sixteenth
century. We should expect, then, that the
pseudo-Bunyan would have the honesty to
admit his shadowy character by giving us some
clue which would enable us to unravel the

mystery. And he has done so." It was always one of the standing problems of Bunyan scholarship why, in Part Two, the Dreamer should at first obtain his information, not from an ocular view, but from hearsay information. He is represented (on page 190) as meeting a certain Mr. Sagacity, who supplies him with news about Christian and his family. Why this peculiar literary artifice? And why the name, Mr. Sagacity? Dr. *Cheese-Paring* has solved the problem by pointing out that the name should be read (after Bunyan's manner) in two halves; it is not Mr. Sagacity, but Mr. Saga-City—an appropriate name, as Canon *Obvious* has pointed out, for the author of *The Holy War*. Mr. Saga-City, then, is simply Bunyan himself, the genuine Bunyan, as opposed to his imitator.

A further indication of the dual authorship is supplied to us later on. Just before reaching the House Beautiful, Christiana and his company meet with a giant called Bloodyman, who is killed by Great-heart. This giant, alone of all the characters in the book, has an alias, and his alias is Giant *Grim*. The word " Grim " puts us on our guard. This is on page 243; on page 254 Christiana's eldest son, Matthew, falls sick, and is cured by a *Pill*. To treat this as a coincidence,

as Mr. *Jettison Cargo* does, is to fly in the face
of modern criticism. Is it not obvious to the
most careless reader that the separation of
" Grim " from " Pill " implies the division of
the work into two halves, with a corresponding
division of authorship?

The duality of origin thus definitely established, it is natural to ask ourselves who was the
imitator who, thus greatly daring, ventured to
continue a work which had achieved such in-
stantaneous popularity? It seems to me that
in the discussion of this question too little
weight has been attached to the theological
viewpoint adopted by the author of Part Two.
Part One is a controversial tract, in which the
favourite theological doctrines of Puritanism
were emphasized again and again. More especially, as we should expect, the author insists on
the theology of Sin, Grace, Redemption, Human
Depravity, and the like.

Thus, one of the first enemies Christian meets
is Mr. Worldly Wiseman, who counsels him to
get rid of his burden by applying to Mr. Legality,
who lives in the village of Morality. Already,
then, the distinction between Grace and the
Law, between Faith and Works, is well marked
(page 13). It is repeated at the Interpreter's

House under the figure of the man sweeping the room (page 25). The Man in the Cage (page 30) expounds the terrible doctrine of Reprobation in all its horrors. Formalist and Hypocrisy (page 35), who climb over the wall instead of coming through the wicket-gate, are evidently typical of that institutional religion which the Puritans despised. The Mosaic Law is contrasted, in the Pauline manner, with the Christian dispensation on page 72. On page 74 Shame uses precisely those arguments against religion which a Churchman of the time might have used against Puritanism. Mr. Talkative's error on the method of discovering the effect of Saving Grace is one which it would take an acute Calvinist theologian to follow (page 84 and following). "Our parson, Mr. Two-tongues," on page 104, is a polemical hit worthy of Prynne himself. The whole book, in fact, is a tract, directed not merely against worldliness but against the theological opponents of Puritanism, whatever their colour.

In Part Two all this has disappeared. There is indeed (on pages 232 sqq.) a long disquisition about Justification, but the whole argument turns on the source of it, not on the manner of it, which was the *crux* of Reformation theology.

Apart from that, it is safe to say that the whole
of Part Two is merely a moral allegory, which a
Christian of any denomination might read with
profit. Why does Christian start with a burden,
and Christiana without one, unless the author
of Christiana was less convinced on the subject of
Original Sin than Bunyan himself? Why is
Mercy actually allowed to start on her pilgrimage without any certain conviction at all
(page 202)? How is it that Matthew eats the
Enemy's fruit, and experiences no worse effect
than an internal disorder which it only needs
a purge to put right? Is this Puritanism, with
its stern contrast between religion and worldliness? The figures shown at the Interpreter's
House—the Man with the Muck-rake, for
example—are only moral allegories. Christiana
and Mercy have a bath at the Interpreter's
House, after which they are clothed in white
robes, a clear reference to Baptism; whereas
Christian is only clothed with white robes when
the burden falls off his back at the Cross, an
equally clear reference to " conversion " (pages
33, 228). And so throughout the book.

The author shows traces of Sacramentalism,
not only in the reference to Baptism already
cited, but in the matter of Matthew's purge,

where the prescription is actually given in Latin
—and no wonder. On page 292 reference is
made to St. Ignatius and St. Polycarp, as if
Puritanism cared for extra-Biblical Saints! On
page 325 the pilgrims are adorned with neck-
laces, etc., *before crossing the river*, a very dangerous allusion surely to the doctrine of Merit;
Bunyan's heroes receive no adornment till they
reach the Celestial City. But, above all, there
is a marked difference in the later author's attitude towards the Church of Rome. Giant Pope
has disappeared from the cave in which he met
us on page 66, to be replaced by the colourless
figure of Giant Maul (page 273). And at
Vanity Fair, Mr. Mnason actually tells the
pilgrims that the people there have " of late
been far more moderate " (page 319). Now, we
know that the wares of Rome were sold at Vanity
Fair (page 93). The Second Part of *Pilgrim's
Progress* appeared in 1684; could it have been
argued, by any stretch of the imagination, that
the England of that period was more tolerant
towards Puritanism, and in less danger from
Romish influences? The England of the Test
Act and the Rye House Plot!

These general impressions are fully corrob-
orated by a careful study of the Biblical

references in *Pilgrim's Progress*, for which I am
indebted to my friend, Dr. *Book-worm*. The
complete table, calculated only on the basis of
the references explicitly given in the margin, is
as follows :

	Part I.	Part II.
The Pentateuch .	20	17
Historical Books .	3	5
Job .	11	2
Psalms	22	10
Proverbs .	19	8
Ecclesiastes	4	5
Song of Songs	1	6
Isaias	23	4
Other Major Prophets .	22	8
Minor Prophets .	11	6
Gospels	56	33
Acts .	7	5
Pauline Epistles .	94	32
Catholic Epistles .	17	16
Apocalypse	21	5
Total	331	162

The first thought which will strike any reader
of the above statistics is that Part Two was
written by somebody who did not know his Bible
nearly as well as Bunyan. (The two parts are
practically equal in length.) But a more careful
scrutiny shows even more interesting results.
Part One quotes the Bible twice as often as
Part Two. To preserve the proportion, we

should expect roughly two quotations from each
division of the Bible in Part One to one in Part
Two. Observe, then, that the Pentateuch, with
its legal and ceremonial associations, the Law of
Moses, from which the Puritan boasts of having
been set free, is almost *equally* represented in
Part Two (20 : 17). Conversely the Major
Prophets, with their constant insistence upon
the insufficiency of human righteousness, show
a miserable twelve as against forty-five; and
Isaias in particular, a favourite author with
St. Paul, only four as against twenty-three. The
Song of Songs, more frequently used by Catholic
than by Protestant writers, is actually quoted
six times in Part Two, only once in Part One.
With the Epistles it is the same story. St. Paul,
upon whom the Reformers so largely rested
their case, is quoted nearly three times as often
in Part One as in Part Two, whereas the Catholic
Epistles only show a difference of seventeen as
against sixteen. These last statistics are even
more telling when itemised. If you isolate
Romans, Ephesians, Galatians and Hebrews as
the Epistles which deal most directly with the
theology of Grace and of Faith, you will find
that they are alluded to fifty-six times in Part
One, only nineteen times in Part Two ; whereas

the Epistle of St. James (" an Epistle of straw,"
as Luther bluntly called it) is quoted twice in
Part One, four times in Part Two. Finally, the
Apocalypse, beloved of Puritan writers, appears
in the margin of Part One four times more
frequently than in the margin of Part Two.

Bishop *While-on-the-one-hand* has taught us
that it is a fatal mistake to theorize in advance
of your data. But I do not feel that I shall be
false to his maxim when I say that Part Two of
Pilgrim's Progress was not written by a Puritan
at all. Every indication shows that it was
written, although probably not by a Catholic,
by an Anglican with tendencies in the Catholic
direction, perhaps one who only waited for the
Duke of York's accession to come out as a
supporter of the Old Religion. The facts given
above warrant no other conclusion.

At least, as Canon *Obvious* admits, it was " a
man of a very different stamp." Or—is it
possible that we ought to quarrel with the gender
he uses? After all, the second half of *Pilgrim's
Progress* is concerned with Christiana, not with
Christian. It shows, throughout, an interest in
match-making which is hardly credible in a
male mind. Of female characters in Part One
there are only five (assuming that Prudence,

Piety, and Charity are an interpolation), and of these, four are bad, only one good. In Part Two no less than seventeen meet us in the course of the story, seven bad and ten good. Let the reader turn to page 293. He will find that in that passage Great-heart launches out into a panegyric upon women, " to take away their reproach." After a very extraordinary allusion to Galatians iv and Genesis iii, he traces the influence of women in the Gospels with the avowed object of showing that they were ahead of the other sex from end to end of the story. It is my own belief, though one which I offer with all due reserve to the public, that this is the true reading of the problem. The fortunes of Christiana, strange as it may seem, were foisted upon the world by a woman, jealous for the credit of her own sex, and an Anglican, equally jealous for the reputation of a much-maligned and recently persecuted Church.

VIII

THE AUTHORSHIP
OF
" IN MEMORIAM "

VIII

THE AUTHORSHIP OF
"IN MEMORIAM"

WHY SHAKESPEARE more than anybody else?

The problem "Who wrote *In Memoriam?*" is one of the most interesting and most complicated in literary history; and it is safe to say that it has not hitherto received the attention it deserved. Everybody is familiar with the outlines of it. Hallam died in 1833, and the poem which professes to be his epicedium did not see the light until 1850. What is the explanation of this monstrous interval? Further, when the poem originally appeared, it was accorded a doubtful reception, and was attributed by some critics (a very significant fact) to a feminine hand. Mr. Nicholson has familiarized us with the verdict of one reviewer in particular, who suggested that it was in all probability composed by the widow of some military man. It was only later that Tennyson stepped in, claimed the poem as his own, and gave it the reputation which it holds at present. The question naturally suggests itself, did Tennyson really write it, or was he screening somebody else? If we adopt the latter view, it will be necessary to urge some sufficient motive for a literary imposition so audacious and so persistent.

One looks, naturally, for a cryptogram. And here a most impressive fact meets us at the very outset of the inquiry. Give the letters their natural value as Greek numerals : that is, make A=1, E=5, I=10, M=40, N=50, O=70, R=100. The letters of *In Memoriam* thus work out at 10+50+40+5+40+70+100+10+1+40, cyphers which on a careful computation add up to 366, the number of days in the full year ! Scarcely less significant is the result if we take the natural values of the English alphabet, starting with A=0, B=1, C=2, etc. The letters of *In Memoriam* on this reckoning give you 8+13+12+4+12+14+17+8+0+12, and these ten cyphers add up to 100 ! Again, if you give the vowels their natural values as a separate series, this time making A=1, E=2, etc., you find that the vowels IEIOA represent 3+2+3+4+1, cyphers which add up to the mystical number

13. Adding 100 to 13 (for want of anything better to do), you arrive at the number 113, and immediately turn to the 113th canto of the poem to see if it holds any secret for posterity. Is it possible that the cryptographer will have betrayed, by some tiny awkwardness of phrase, some tiny evidence of strained writing, the line in this canto which contains the clue?

The search is not a difficult one. Few readers of the poem can have failed to note the artificial effect of the 11th line :

A potent voice of Parliament—

why OF Parliament, instead of IN Parliament? The latter, surely, is what any author would naturally have written. Is not the change from " in " to " of " just such a change as might have been forced on him, not by any demands of literary appropriateness, but by the desire to select two particular letters *which would complete a particular message in cypher ?* It might be a fresh numerical cypher, it might be merely anagrammatical. . . . One has to play with various possibilities, and then an anagram leaps quite suddenly into view. What it is we shall see later. For the present, let us simply note that the 11th line of the 113th canto of *In Memoriam* can be read anagrammatically, and when so read gives a thoroughly sensational message.

It also (as will be seen later) indicates unmistakably that it is the *last* of a series of cryptograms. As an hypothesis, then, it may be worth considering the possibility that it is the last of a series of 11, which will involve verse 1 of canto *x*, verse 2 of canto *y*, and so on. It would be easy to construct an artificial series for the purpose (e.g., 13, 23, etc.), but a natural series is not so easily arrived at. It is here that a certain amount of intricate mathematical thinking is involved, the details of which we spare the reader, giving only the conclusions. It will be seen that the series is a real and natural one, though sufficiently abstruse to be worthy of an accomplished cryptographer such as the poet we are dealing with.

It runs as follows :

$$
\begin{array}{ccc}
 & 1 & = & 1 \\
* & * & & * \\
1 \times 2 + 1 & = & 3 \\
* & * & & * \\
2 \times 2 + 2 & = & 6 \\
6 \times 2 + 1 & = & 13 \\
* & * & & * \\
3 \times 2 + 3 & = & 9 \\
9 \times 2 + 2 & = & 20 \\
20 \times 2 + 1 & = & 41 \\
* & * & & *
\end{array}
$$

$$4 \times 2 + 4 \ = \ 12$$
$$12 \times 2 + 3 \ = \ 27$$
$$27 \times 2 + 2 \ = \ 56$$
$$56 \times 2 + 1 \ = \ 113$$

Taking the formula as $xy + z$, it will be seen that y is always 2, that z is in turn 1, 2, 1, 3, 2, 1, 4, 3, 2, 1; that x is in turn 1, 2, 3, 4, at the beginning of the division, and in the rest of the division is simply a repetition of the last total reached.

On our present hypothesis, then (for it is so far a hypothesis) we shall expect to find a cryptogram (in the form of an anagram) in the following lines: line 1 of canto 1, line 2 of canto 3, line 3 of canto 6, line 4 of canto 13, and so on till we get to line 11 of canto 113. Let us give the results of this speculation :—

1.	1	I held it truth, with him who sings.
3.	2	O priestess in the vaults of death.
6.	3	And common is the commonplace.
13.	4	Her place is empty, fall like these.
9.	5	So draw him home to those that mourn.
20.	6	And weep the fulness from the mind.
41.	7	Thy changes; here upon the ground.
12.	8	And leave the cliffs, and haste away.
27.	9	Nor, what may count itself as blest.
56.	10	Such splendid purpose in his eyes.
113.	11	A potent voice of Parliament.

Before we go any farther we may at once comment upon a corroborative symptom. Omit

the first two and the last two of these lines, and
the intervening lines give us a perfect single
acrostic. It runs, " Ah Satan ! " Somebody
clearly felt that he or she was being tempted to
violate conscience, and registered a protest in
this way. We shall see that the seven lines of
the acrostic have a common thread running
through them.

Anagrams are slow work, and a " Word
Making and Word Taking " outfit is recommended to the beginner. The letters of " I held
it truth, with him who sings " yield, with a little
arrangement, the following rather intriguing
result: " Who is writing this? H.M. luteth
hid." It was, no doubt, the word " harp " in
the next line of the poem that suggested to the
cryptographer the rather fanciful word " luteth."
The implication is plain enough ; the author of
this poem is not its reputed author ; somebody
described as H.M. is really writing the poem,
but prefers to remain hidden, that is anonymous.
So far we have not much to go upon in the way
of positive information ; after all, there must
have been plenty of people writing in 1850
who would answer to the required initials. We
turn on, then, impatiently to canto 3, line 2,
and are met with a startling announcement.

" O priestess in the vaults of death " reads quite unmistakably " V.R.I. the poetess. Alf T. has no duties." Astounding—impossible ! Yet there it is in black and white ; there is no getting over the documentary evidence. English sovereigns had not yet adopted the imperial title (the Mutiny was yet to come), but already it must have been designed *in petto*. There was only one person in England who could be designated indifferently " H.M." or " V.R.I."

And yet, is it so extraordinary? Has anybody read Queen Victoria's published diaries without being conscious of a note of domesticity, a note of resignation, a note of common human pathos, which finds its very counterpart in the stanzas of *In Memoriam?* There was, after all, something to be said for the critic who suspected feminine authorship. But at that period of our history, though a woman might write poetry, a queen might not publish it. It was necessary to conceal the secret as if it had been a guilty one, or the consequences might have been international. The arrangement, then, clearly, was that the work should be published anonymously, but that Tennyson, then a rising poet, should be prepared if necessary to cast veracity to the winds, and shoulder the onus of authorship. It

was a patriot's act; and perhaps something of
the moral struggle which it involves is reflected
in the next cryptogram, which is in Latin.
"And common is the commonplace" (a line
which many of us have felt before now to be
something less than Elizabethan in its quality)
is after all only an ingenious cloak for the Latin
motto "Pie hoc nomen clam commodans. T.",
that is to say, "Devotedly lending this name in
secret. T." The man who wrote thus had faced
a moral problem, and had risen superior to it.

It would be necessary for Tennyson to "lend
his name" if either of two things happened—if
discovery of the real authorship threatened, or
if the anonymous appearance of the book should
prove injurious to its sales. Which motive in
fact became operative? The next cryptogram
leaves us in no doubt, and indeed casts a rather
sinister light on the whole proceeding. Tennyson had no doubt been studying Bacon as a
master of cryptographic method; and he will
have been struck, as all of us will have been
struck, at the singular ease with which you may
find cryptograms in the works of the Eliza-
bethans, *because any sort of spelling will do*. Imitat-
ing, then, the crude orthography of Gloriana's
period, he has delicately indicated the motive

which was responsible, at least in part, both for the original publication of the poem and for the invocation of Tennysonian patronage. " Her place is empty, fall like these " can be nothing other than " Her Maiesty lacks pelf. I'le help. TE."

It will already have occurred to the ingenious reader that the letter T left over in the third, and the letters TE left over in the fourth cryptogram, are a sort of rudimentary signature, which (by a pretty piece of ingenuity) adds one letter to itself each time it occurs. This is true only of the seven lines which form the acrostic " Ah, Satan," and consequently they stop at " TENNYSO," just short of the complete signature. The fifth and sixth are mere repetitions of the message which the earlier cypher has given us. " So draw him home to those that mourn " is to be read (no doubt in playful allusion to the May Queen) as " O Mother, I'm H.M.'s shadow-author! TEN." " And weep the fulness from the mind " is meant for a mock warning to the reviewers of the poem, suitably couched in the words, " Who pummels Faith-Defender? TENN." One recognizes, in the choice of the verb, Tennyson's own love for vigorous English,

Alas, that our minds should be built on such a mercenary pattern! We naturally ask, was this generous loan of his name to bring Tennyson no reward from the real authoress of the poem? History supplies us with a painfully distinct answer—Tennyson became Poet Laureate in 1850, the very year of *In Memoriam's* publication! It is no doubt to this recognition of his services that he alludes, with what some will think doubtful taste, in the next cryptogram. We have done our best to find some other anagrammatic equivalent for the words "Thy changes; here upon the ground," but the unfortunate fact defeats us. There can be no doubt that we are to understand it as meaning "Oh hurrah! Nest-egg pouched! TENNY." Let us pass hastily over this lapse from dignity, pausing only to admire the characteristically keen appreciation of Nature which the metaphor shows. And, indeed, the recognition was not undeserved, for it appears that the whole conception of the artifice originated with Tennyson: so at least the eighth cryptogram gives us to understand. "And leave the cliffs, and haste away" can hardly stand for anything but "La! What a safe device Alf had! TENNYS." He had indeed burrowed deep, but he should not have trusted to the impenetrability of his armour so far as to give way to these regrettable outbursts of exultation.

What, then, was the original purpose of the poem? Queen Victoria did not know Arthur Hallam, and it is clear that the initials were merely chosen in order to lend plausibility to the story that it was Tennyson's work. Was it, then, some quite imaginary person whose death evoked this touching threnody? We might have remained in the dark, were it not for one final disclosure of the cypher-lines. The ninth cryptogram is more difficult to read than the others, because more allusively expressed, but there can be no doubt of the true version. " Nor, what may count itself as blest " must be " Let A.H. act for W. Lamb's suit. TENNY-SO "—or possibly " Let W. Lamb suit, cast for A. H. TENNYSO." The metaphor will be sartorial on the former supposition, histrionic on the latter; in any case there can be no doubt as to the hero. William Lamb was the family name of that Lord Melbourne who was Queen Victoria's first and favourite Prime Minister. Mr. Lytton Strachey has given abundant evidence of the warm respect and admiration, something half filial and half romantic, which

the young Queen felt for Lord Melbourne.
When did he die? In the November of 1848, a
date which exactly suits the circumstances of
the poem. It enhances our respect for Queen
Victoria's poetic gifts when we reflect that
this long and intricate work was the fruit of
little more than a year's labour.

The tenth cryptogram raises the question—
If Victoria was the authoress of the poem, how
was it that Tennyson came to supply the cypher?
There must, it seems, have been collaboration
here, and there could be few more generous
tributes than that which is paid in the words
"Such splendid purpose in his eyes." For
these, when read according to the cryptographer's intention, give you: "She lisp'd in
sinuous cyphers deep "—the praise is the praise
of Victoria, but the voice is the voice of Tennyson. And yet the man who could write such
a line as that could take pride in signing himself
at the conclusion of his cryptographic message:
"A potent voice of Parliament," which, it need
hardly be pointed out, stands for "Alf, poet-
pen to Victoria. Amen."

The chain of evidence, then, may be summed
up as follows:

1.	1	Who is writing this? H.M. luteth hid.
3.	2	V.R.I. the poetess. Alf T. has no duties.
6.	3	Pie hoc nomen clam commodans. T.
13.	4	Her Maiesty lacks pelf; I'le help. TE.
9.	5	O Mother, I'm H.M.'s shadow-author! TEN.
20.	6	Who pummels Faith-Defender? TENN.
41.	7	Oh, hurrah! Nest-egg pouched! TENNY.
12.	8	La! What a safe device Alf had! TENNYS.
27.	9	Let A.H. act for W. Lamb's suit. TENNYSO.
56.	10	She lisp'd in sinuous cyphers deep.
113.	11	Alf, poet-pen to Victoria. Amen.

There is much, no doubt, still to be explained as to the personal allusions of *In Memoriam*: some, no doubt, deliberately put in as a blind, others referring in a veiled way to incidents in Lord Melbourne's career. But, in the face of evidence such as this, will anyone attempt to rack the long arm of coincidence so as to make it cover this extraordinary series of cryptograms? If so, he has the ostrich-mind that cannot, because it will not, acquiesce in the assured results of modern enquiry.

Why Shakespeare more than anybody else?

IX

MATERIALS
FOR A
BOSWELLIAN PROBLEM

IX

MATERIALS FOR A BOSWELLIAN
PROBLEM

IT IS a circumstance little creditable to the
ingenuity of modern criticism that a work
like Boswell's *Johnson* should have been thumbed
for over a century by learned and simple,
without any question being raised as to the
sources from which so remarkable a book was
compiled. The name of Boswell, like that of
Homer, Shakespeare, or Luke, is no doubt a
convenient symbol; and to discard its use
altogether would be pedantic, and possibly
misleading. But, while we are content to use
the name, we must not allow the superficial
unity of the work to which it is prefixed blind
us to the fact that it is a compilation—a compilation from sources widely different in their
manner of treatment, and, to some extent, in
their portrayal of the facts.

In such cases it is sometimes urged that the probabilities are, *ceteris paribus*, against a composite authorship; that scissors were less cheap, and paste was less adhesive, in ancient days than in our own; that, for all the hundreds of sources which scholars have postulated to subserve their critical theories, no single one has ever been discovered existing in its uncomposite form; that (in short) the traditional authorship of any work has a *prescriptive right*, and holds the field until such time as sure arguments can be produced to disprove it. Whatever may be the value of such contentions (and they are contentions which have found little favour among scholars these last hundred years), they clearly do not apply to the matter in hand. For (1) the age of Boswell was an age of literary forgeries; we remember Chatterton, we remember Macpherson's *Ossian*, we remember the *History of Formosa*. (2) The age of Boswell was an age of pseudepigraphy; does not the work itself describe how Rolt went over to Dublin and printed Akenside's *Pleasures of the Imagination* bodily under his own name; how a firm of Booksellers commissioned one Shiels to write the *Lives of the Poets*, and then got leave from Theophilus Cibber to

write " Mr. Cibber " on the title-page, so that
the work might pass for Colley Cibber's production? Let it be observed, too, that Johnson
wrote a preface for one of Rolt's books, and
employed Shiels as an amanuensis; pseudepigraphy, therefore, had eaten into the very
heart of the Johnsonian circle. (3) The age
of Boswell was an age of literary patchwork.
Johnson himself supplied lines to Goldsmith's
Traveller and to his *Deserted Village;* and (conversely) he printed among his Lives of the Poets,
without acknowledgment, a notice of Young
written by one Croft. There can scarcely have
been any coterie so baffling in its literary ramifi-
cations, so unscrupulous in its literary conscience, as the coterie which mystified the
public with the *Letters of Junius*, and bam-
boozled it with the *Ballad of Harthacnute.*

The presumption, then, is actually in favour
of a composite authorship for Boswell. And
no reader who has once dallied with the thought
can fail to observe, even upon the most cursory
perusal, three different divisions running through
the work. It will be as well to distinguish
these at once, before considering the detailed
proofs of their independence. Of course, these
three are only the main divisions; when you

have disentangled them, you are in the position of one who has unpicked the strands of a rope, without dissolving these, in turn, into their component fibres. When we speak of "sources," we do not feel bound to mention every isolated tributary that has fed them.

(1) You find, first of all, a plain, unvarnished biography of the alleged Doctor, careful to name the informants from which its matter is derived, incorporating large numbers of apparently genuine letters, some few of which are addressed to James Boswell, Esq. It is doubtful whether the author of this document had ever met or even seen Johnson. The few passages which begin " He told me " or " He communicated to me " are probably taken wholesale from some other source. It is characteristic of this document that in its earlier part it always refers to its hero as " Johnson," unlike the " We "-passages, which dignify him with the title of Doctor in 1763, two years before his doctorate was given him by Dublin (p. 248, etc.[1]).

(2) You enter at once into a new atmosphere when you encounter the " We "-passages. Here

[1] The page references are to the " Everyman " edition throughout.

you have a document which was apparently kept in diary form, recording few facts, numerous conversations; distinguishing each of these by the day of the month, not merely by the year. The author was (or professes to have been) on terms of daily intimacy with Johnson and his friends.

(3) Interspersed with these are extracts from yet a third document, written in dramatic or dialogue form throughout. The subject is introduced by a short rubric, and the remarks made upon it are prefaced by the names of the interlocutors, turn and turn about, as in a play. A typical instance will begin as follows: " I introduced the subject of toleration. JOHNSON. Every society has a right to preserve publick peace " and so on. It is characteristic of this document that it records no events, only scattered utterances or *logia* of the great man; that it assigns no dates to them, and indeed has been used by the compiler at haphazard, without due reference to dating; that it records Johnson's arguments with his friends, not with his natural enemies, such as Wilkes and Gibbon.

For purposes of convenience, I shall call the author of the first document C, or the Chronicler; that of the We-passages W; and that of the third document D, or the Dialogist. We must further make allowance for at least two Redactors (R 1 and R 2), who have reduced the whole composition to its present shape. The following table will give some idea of the distribution of these sources, beginning with Vol. I :

C. Pages 1-240, 297-311, 320-341, 381-407, 447-451, etc.

W. Pages 241-270, 285-296, 312-314, 342-365, 378-380, 425-446, etc.

D. Pages 271-284, 315-319, 366-378, 408-424, etc.

It must be observed, however, that isolated passages from D are let in, here and there, in the middle of C or W extracts, their peculiar form lending itself to this treatment. There are between thirty and forty of these D-insertions in the pages ascribed to C and W above.

The discrepancies between C and D are manifest, though not usually important. Thus, in C Rolt is credited with a " Dictionary of Trade and Commerce " which becomes a " Dictionary of Commerce " merely, in D (Vol. 1, pp. 221, 545), and C's " Universal Visiter " is " The Universal Visitor " in D (Vol. I, pp. 186, 546). But occasionally the differences are more significant. Thus we read in a D-insertion, Vol. I, p. 28, of Jorden, Johnson's Oxford tutor:

" He was a very worthy man, *but a heavy man, and I did not profit much by his instructions.* . . . The first day after I came to College, I waited upon him, and then stayed away four. On the sixth, Mr. Jorden asked me why I had not attended. I answered, I had been sliding in Christ Church meadow. BOSWELL: That, sir, was great fortitude of mind. JOHNSON: No, Sir, stark insensibility."

The same incident is recorded in quite different terms by C, which here incorporates some reminiscences of Dr. Warton (Vol. I, p. 162):

" He much regretted that his first tutor was dead, for whom *he seemed to entertain the greatest regard.* He said, I had once been a whole morning sliding in Christ Church meadows, and missed his lecture in logick. After dinner he sent for me to his room. I expected a sharp rebuke for my idleness, and *went with a beating heart.* When we were seated, he told me he had sent for me to drink a glass of wine with him, and to tell me he was not angry with me for missing his lecture."

It will be noticed that D, here as always, is

at pains to introduce a *logion* of the Doctor's, probably at the expense of truth. A reminiscence has been turned into a retort. At the same time, it seems clear that D did not depend on C here, but that the two presuppose a common original. In other passages, it would appear that D gives us the correct version, while C has improved it out of all recognition. So a conversation on Foote, the mimic, is thus recorded by D (Vol. I, p. 369) :

" BOSWELL : Did he not think of exhibiting you, sir? JOHNSON : Sir, fear restrained him ; he knew I would have broken his bones."

Now let us observe what C has made out of this chance remark (Vol. I, p. 517) :

" Foote . . . had resolved to imitate Johnson on the stage. . . . Johnson being informed of his intention, and being at dinner at Mr. Thomas Davies' the bookseller, from whom I had the story, he asked Mr. Davies what was the price of a common oak stick ; and being answered sixpence, Why then, sir, (said he) give me leave to send your servant to purchase me a shilling one."

I fancy that if we still possessed X, the lost original of C and D, we should find it a document considerably more colourless than either of its descendants.

The interdependence of D and W is equally loose. We may instance the following comparison of W (Vol. I, p. 258) with D (Vol. II, p. 176):

W. " Campbell is not always rigidly careful of truth in his conversation, but I do not believe there is anything of this carelessness in his books. Campbell is a good man, a pious man. I am afraid he has not been in the inside of a church for many years, but he never passes a church without pulling off his hat. That shows that he has good principles."

D. " I do not know that Campbell ever lied with pen and ink, but you could not entirely depend on anything he told you in conversation. . . . However, I loved Campbell: he was a solid orthodox man: he had a reverence for religion. Though defective in practice, he was religious in principle."

Redactor 2 has altered the present tense to the past in D, since he found the incident inserted under a date when Campbell was no longer alive; but this is, without question, a doublet of the same *logion*. The common source here is more likely to have been oral than written. The same consideration arises from a comparison of Vol. I, p. 422, with

Vol. II, p. 470. In the former place, D has " Promiscuous hospitality is not the way to gain real influence. . . . No, sir, the way to make sure of power and influence is, by lending money to your neighbours at a small interest, or perhaps at no interest at all, and having their bonds in your possession." W has the version, " No, sir, you will have much more influence by giving or lending money where it is wanted, than by hospitality." The discrepancies sometimes extend beyond mere turns of phrase ; thus W (II, 55) reports Johnson as saying of Mrs. Rudd, the actress, " Boswell is in the right ; I should have visited her myself, were it not that they have now a trick of putting everything into the newspapers," whereas D (II, 235) has : " JOHNSON : Fifteen years ago I should have gone to see her. SPOTTISWOODE : Because she was fifteen years younger? JOHNSON : No, sir ; but now they have a trick of putting everything into the newspapers."

Other doublets between W and D (e.g. I, 345 and 411 ; I, 277 and II, 54 ; II, 268 and 530) are less interesting. On the whole, it is probable that D is a better representative than W of their common original, which I will call Y. For instance, W has the following (II,

167) : " Talking of ghosts, he said, It is wonderful that 5,000 years have now elapsed since the creation of the world, and still it is undecided whether or not there has ever been an instance of the spirit of any person appearing after death. All argument is against it, but all belief is for it. He said, John Wesley's conversation is good." Naturally the reader is at a loss to follow the transition of thought. Let him turn to D's account on p. 213 of Vol. II : " Of John Wesley, he said he can talk well on any subject. BOSWELL : Pray, sir, what has he made of his story of a ghost? JOHNSON : Why, sir, he believes it, but not on sufficient authority. He did not take time enough to examine the girl. MISS SEWARD : What, sir ! About a ghost? JOHNSON : Yes, madam ; this is a question which, after 5,000 years, is still undecided." D, in spite of its erratic use by the compiler, has obviously succeeded in giving the *logion* its true setting.

Discrepancies between C and W are less numerous. But the following instance will suffice to prove it. C had the words (I. 109) " Mr. Shiels, who *partly wrote* the Lives of the Poets to which the name of Cibber is attached " ; and Redactor 2, conscious of a doublet,

attempted to soften it down by inserting the
words " as we shall hereafter see " after the
word " who." Alas for human prudence!
He had neglected to observe that W's statement (II. 23) was something quite different:
" He told us, that the book entitled the Lives
of the Poets, by Mr. Cibber, was *entirely compiled* by Mr. Shiels." The two statements are
not, of course, inconsistent, but the allegation
contained differs in the two cases.

And now, what of the *Journal of a Tour to the
Hebrides?* This, too, is manifestly a composite
document, but there is none of C's work in it,
except a passage which has been borrowed from
him by a We-passage in the *Journal*, so curiously
that it deserves to be set out at full length:

Life, Vol. II, p. 614.	*Journal* (Introduction).
His figure was large and well formed	His person was large, robust, I may say approaching to the gigantick, and grown unwieldy from corpulency.
and his countenance of the cast of an ancient statue;	His countenance was naturally of the cast of an ancient statue,
yet his appearance was rendered strange and somewhat uncouth, by convulsive cramps, by the scars of that distemper which it was once imagined the royal touch could cure,	but somewhat disfigured by the scars of that evil

which, it was formerly imagined, the royal touch could cure . . . |
| and by a slovenly mode of dress, | |

He had the use only of one eye, yet, so much does the mind govern, and even supply, the deficiency of organs, that his visual perceptions as far as they extended	His sight had always been somewhat weak, yet, so much does mind govern, and even supply, the deficiency of organs that his perceptions
were uncommonly quick and accurate.	were uncommonly quick and accurate.

The most casual observer cannot fail to note that it is the *Journal* which has borrowed from C, and not *vice versa*. The later scribe has exaggerated, with the natural tendency of the human mind towards mythology, the grossness of the Doctor's person, and, omitting the loss of the one eye, he has gratuitously implied that the sight of the other was weak.

But, if C has deserted us, W and D persist, though it is highly doubtful whether the W and D of the *Journal* are, respectively, the W and D of the *Life*. On the contrary, verbal resemblances occur between D of the *Life* and W of the *Journal*, e.g. " The noblest prospect that (which) a Scotchman ever sees, is the high road that leads him to England (London)." The *logion* is referred by D to a party at the Mitre, by W to a scene which purports to have taken place at Edinburgh Castle (*Life*, Vol. I, p. 264; *Journal*, under November 10). On the other hand, the *logion* about Walmsley and Toryism is verbally identical in W (*Life*, Vol. I, p. 267) and in a We-passage of the *Journal* (under November 10). Johnson's contention that Swift could not have written the *Tale of a Tub*, because it was too good, is recorded in the *Life* by D (I. 280) and by W (I. 530), and also by a We-passage of the *Journal* (under August 16). It is safest, then, to assume that both the documents used in the Journal owed some (at least) of their inspiration to Y, the common original of D and W in the *Life;* I have designated these *Journal*-sources by the letters small d and small w.

It is plain that D and d do not depend entirely on a common source. Thus D (I.510) has " If a man were to go by chance at the same time with Burke under a shed, to shun a shower, he would say, This is an extraordinary man." Whereas d substitutes (under August 15) " Burke, sir, is such a man that if you met him for the first time in the street where you were stopped by a drove of oxen, and you and he stepped aside to take shelter but for five minutes, he'd talk to you in such a manner that, when you parted, you would say, This is an extraordinary man." This latter version appears to be corrupt—one does not take shelter from oxen ;

the former may perhaps point to a verse original (cf. the alliteration of " shed, to shun a shower "). On the other hand, the resemblances between W and w are clearly marked (cf. I. 485 with *Journal* of October 14, II. 220 with *Journal* of August 20).

Perhaps the most instructive doublet of all is the famous *logion* which compares a ship to a prison. The *Journal* for August 31, gives this : " No man will be a sailor who has contrivance enough to get himself into a jail ; for being in a ship is being in a jail, with the chance of being drowned." And under September 23 the same document gives " The man in a jail has more room, better food, and commonly better company, AND IS IN SAFETY." C in the *Life* (I. 215) reproduces both these *logia*, but omits the words " and is in safety " in the second. A footnote gives references to the passages in the *Journal*. Elsewhere in the *Life* (I. 612), W gives us the following : " A ship is worse than a gaol (*sic*). There is, in a gaol, better air, better company, better conveniency of every kind ; and a ship has the additional disadvantage of being in danger." It would be hard to find a more interesting instance of literary transmission. There was, in the original source from which C and W borrowed, a *logion* which insisted that a prison was only equal to a ship in respect of discomfort, and superior to it in respect of safety. C and W have their respective versions of it. Then d, who has access to C and W, borrows the two quotations from C, and adds, from W, the rider " and is in safety." Finally, Redactor 2 confuses the trail by giving us references to the *Journal* in footnotes to the *Life*.

We may now represent our results in the following tabular form:

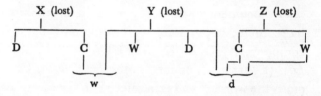

It would be interesting, but somewhat laborious, to examine the characteristic differences between these various sources in the picture which they give of their hero. It is certain, for example, that those passages which represent Dr. Johnson as favourable to the Catholic religion are due entirely to D (cf. I. 375, 376-377, 411, 484; II. 520), whereas his true attitude was on the whole one of repugnance, as

may be seen from W's portrayal of him (I. 610;
II. 14; II. 289). The reference in II. 14
appears, indeed, in the dialogue form, and
might have been attributed to D, but the exact
mark of date shows that it is a We-passage:
probably the word " said " has dropped out
after the word " Johnson." Compare especially
Johnson's attitude on the Invocation of Saints,
as reported in II. 289, with his defence of the
doctrine in two of the D-passages. Again, D
tends to give us the impression that Dr. Johnson
was something of a temperance fanatic (I. 436,
439; II. 29, 177, 233, 239); whereas W shows
that if anything he was in favour of drinking
(II. 39, 125, 270, 275). But it is not always
easy to trace these discrepancies to their
true source. For example, Johnson's famous
account of the tour is called *A Journey to the
Hebrides* in I. 500 (C), 502 (C), 507 (C); II.
189 (D), 232 (D), whereas it is *A Journey
to the Western Islands* in I. 517 (C), 557
(W); II. 73 (C), 103 (W), 127 (W), and
216 (D).

A more serious question naturally presents
itself: How much, in either book, gives us
authentic information; how much is to be
taken with a grain of salt? On the whole, it
may be said that C is a careful narrative,

documented from various sources and giving
a consistent picture of the Doctor's life and
character. Can we say as much for D or
for W? C gives you the picture of a voracious reader and a prolific author, who would
have (one would think) little time for con-
vivial company, or for unnecessary conversation.
Whereas a perusal of D or W conveys the
impression that the man was for ever talking
and hobnobbing with his cronies; he never
pleads an engagement or complains of any
press of work; in short, it is the picture of an
idler. Can the two really be reconciled?
And is there any real evidence that Johnson
was fond of talking? On the contrary, there
is good reason to believe that he was reserved
and shy in company. So at least we read in
a passage probably attributable to C (II. 220),
" Tom Tyers described me the best: Sir (he
said) you are like a ghost; you never speak
till you are spoken to," an estimate which w
repeats under August 20. Can it be said
that Johnson, in D or in W, ever waits till he
is spoken to? On the contrary, it seems
impossible for anybody else to get a word in
edgeways.

We all know how frequently *bons mots* are attributed to Dr. Johnson or to Sydney Smith, when in fact their origin is much later or much earlier. If some of the *bons mots* attributed to Dr. Johnson are spurious, why not all? The more so since (as I have abundantly shown) the exact form of expression in them and even the point conveyed by them is often differently represented by the different sources. It seems evident upon a closer view that C gives us a true, though not a very interesting biography, whose hero is an awkward recluse, distinguished only as a man of letters; that subsequent legends have grown up round his name (represented by W and D), which would represent him as a master of the social arts and graces. To emphasize the distinction between the two pictures, I need only notice that C in II. 614 tells us Johnson " when he rode had no command or direction of his horse, but was carried as if in a balloon "; yet W has the effrontery to print the words " I told him I had been to see Johnson ride upon three horses " ![1]

---

[1] A friend has suggested to me that this "Johnson" is someone else of the same name; surely this is mere special pleading. Everywhere else in the *Life* the name "Johnson" has only one meaning.

And if we are to write down W and D in the *Life* as apocryphal, what of the *Journal of a Tour to the Hebrides?* Can we suppose that this has any foundation in fact? Dr. Johnson himself, of course, wrote an account of such a Journey, but it is improbable that anyone was meant to take this seriously, in an age when bogus travels were so commonly published. The only passage in the *Life* which suggests that Dr. Johnson did actually make such a tour is a brief statement on p. 491 of Vol. 1, supported by a few letters supposed to have passed between Johnson and his friend. (There is no allusion to it in letters to any other person.) The passage on p. 491 is of a highly suspicious character; it definitely states that Johnson arrived in Scotland on August 18th, whereas the *Journal* brings him to Edinburgh on August 14th. Is it not clear that we are in the realm of mythology? The more so as the *Journal* itself abounds in improbabilities. It relates, for example, the whole Flora Macdonald saga as if it were fact. *The Tour to the Hebrides*, if I may so express myself, is a *tour de force*. What (men asked themselves) would have happened if Dr. Johnson, the well-known hater of the Scots, had actually made a pilgrimage

North of the Border? What would have been his reactions on seeing the Scots at home? Such speculations tend to clothe themselves, before long, in the dress of reported facts. So often had Dr. Johnson made merry over the theories of Lord Monboddo—let us bring the two men meet face to face, nay, let us make Lord Monboddo offer the shelter of his roof to Dr. Johnson! So, insensibly, the myth builds itself up, aided by the fact that there was little accurate knowledge, in those days, to correct the fancy picture given of the Hebrides. It is a fantasia; and indeed it may be questioned whether the whole conception of Dr. Johnson has not been influenced by that of Dr. Syntax.

Although it is highly doubtful, as we have seen, whether Samuel Johnson really uttered any of those numerous *dicta* with which the credulity or carelessness of contemporary writers has credited him, we must not therefore suppose that such a book as Boswell's *Life* has no permanent value. There is a higher truth than that of mere fact; and the portrait which the book gives of its hero, however destitute of an historical foundation, will not cease to be an inspiration to many thoughtful people, and to mould the ideals of posterity. Dr. Johnson will not, perhaps, be so great a figure to our descendants as he was to our forefathers. It is now recognized that the six "amanuenses" whom he employed were, in fact, the authors of the Dictionary which goes by his name, while he himself added little except his name and a few unimportant redactions. Though we cannot positively assert, we can at least give good reasons for suspecting, that *Rasselas* is a skit on the Johnsonian manner, produced by the same lively talent which gave us the Letters of Junius.[1] But Johnson will remain a tradition and a legend, for generations of Englishmen to admire. He will be remembered as one who, with a natural tendency towards ill-health, struggled manfully against the disqualifications imposed upon him by disease; as one who was born in a humble station, yet rose, through the editing of several newspapers, into a position of intimacy with rich men; as a lover of London, and an early patron of its principal restaurants. If the facts of his life are now mostly disputed, and the authenticity of his works largely denied,

---

[1] Rasselas was published " in March or April of 1759," and it can hardly be a coincidence that its title, " Rasselas, Prince of Abyssinia " is the anagram of the words " April, i.e. Ass-season, by Francis."

that is, after all, but the penalty of having matriculated two hundred years ago—it may as well come now, since it would have had to come sooner or later. " Facts," says the Bishop of Much Wenlock in the current number of his Diocesan Magazine, " are only the steam which obscures the mirror of truth."

X

JOTTINGS
FROM A
PSYCHO-ANALYST'S NOTE-BOOK

JOTTINGS FROM A PSYCHO-ANALYST'S NOTE-BOOK

(From the German of Dr. Freud-Struwwelpeter)

CASE I.—Peter ———, aged six, called "Shock-headed Peter" by his friends. He refuses obstinately to cut either his hair or his nails, which have consequently grown to a prodigious extent. His parents, instead of applauding his decision or trying to help him in any way, lose no opportunity of evincing a morbid disgust at his appearance. My first impression was, of course, that he wished he was a girl; but his obstinacy in the matter of the nails seems to discount this theory. I have put him down provisionally as a case of shell-shock, which may be compensating itself in this way: the nails, of course, suggesting shells and his long hair the shock. On the other hand, there is no positive evidence that he has ever been under fire. It is possible that he is merely a

fanatic on the subject of growth—there is such
a thing as vegetative hypertrophy. I have told
the parents that his wishes in the matter must be
rigorously respected; it is the only chance for
him.

Case II.—Frederick ———, aged six. From
his earliest years he gave signs of what was
thought to be " cruelty," catching flies with
considerable agility and then tearing off their
wings. He then proceeded to killing birds, and
—a less unamiable but perhaps not less significant trait—breaking the chairs. It was when
he threw the kitten downstairs that his parents
began to fear there was something amiss; it
was most unfortunate that they did not call in
a psychological expert there and then. For, up
to that point, the perversion was a simple one:
it was simply a gravitation complex. Only a
year or two before he was born, an aunt of his
narrowly escaped witnessing an aviation accident, and the whole idea of flying is therefore
repellent to the boy's subconsciousness. The
flies must be deprived of their wings; the birds,
less easily mutilated, must be killed outright.
His passion even vents itself upon chairs, because
these, too, are designed to prevent human
beings from falling on to the ground. A morbid

curiosity on his part insists that the kitten shall make experiments in aviation. After this, however, a sudden transference seems to have turned him in the direction of flagellomania. He first beat his nurse, Mary ———, who broke down and cried—the worst thing she could have done in the circumstances. His next victim was a dog called Tray—or rather, there was victimisation on both sides, for the dog resented the treatment and bit him, an injury which may have grave results. It is worth observing that the two names " Mary " and " Tray " both contain the letters " ary," which are calculated to suggest the idea of aviation to the subconsciousness. I have directed the discontinuance of the medicine prescribed by the family doctor, since the patient finds it unpalatable.

Case III.—Harriet ———, aged nine, suspected of pyromania; it is unsafe, the mother declares, to leave the house while a box of matches is lying within reach; Harriet immediately starts lighting them, and shows a perverted pleasure in watching them burn, " jumps for joy " is her mother's description. I questioned Harriet as to the sensation she felt; she could only tell me that " when they burn, it is so pretty, they crackle so, and spit, and flame; Mamma, too, often does the same." The grammatical solecism here is very interesting. Mamma, as match-lighter, seems to be identified with the matches themselves. Much harm has been done by the mother and nurse, who have threatened to scold Harriet if the incident recurs. This threat has set up an unusual and probably totemistic complex in the child's mind; she is constantly under the hallucination that two cats, kept by the family, are urging her not to light matches. I have suggested that these cats should be got rid of, reminding the mother that πῦρ is Greek for fire, which might make them responsible for the arson-suggestion—or it may be an inversion, " water " being suggested by way of " pussy-foot." The mother seems unconvinced. Possibly, of course, Harriet wishes she had been born a boy, and this is her compensation for smoking.

Case IV.—A whole family of boys, Edward, William, and Arthur ———, used to cause considerable trouble by running after and laughing at a " coloured " gentleman living in the neighbourhood. In itself, the case seems to be an ordinary Japhet-complex: there is no American ancestry, but the patriotic sense seems to have over-developed, as Edward is described as having "waved his little flag" when following the unfortunate gentleman, which seems to give something of a political colour to his action. (All the boys have their play-instinct over-developed; William's hoop may have suggested marriage to him, and so given him the lynching-impulse.) No great harm would have been done, if the case had not been handled by a totally unqualified man, Dr. Agrippa ———, a neighbour of the family. He seems to have resorted to the fatal policy of argument: " Boys, leave the blackamoor alone, for if he tries with all his might, he cannot change from black to white." The method is certainly futile, and even the facts may be disputed (cf. the case of Clarkson Thomas, in Louisiana, who is said to have attained a perceptibly grey tint). His remonstrances being disregarded, he proceeded to the very drastic step of administering an ink-bath ! It is too late for me to do anything, and whatever symptoms the boys may develop later either of the Japhet-tendency or of reluctance to pay income tax, must be attributed intirely to the interference of one of those quack doctors who do so much harm to the profession.

Case V.—(name suppressed): a man in
middle life, suffering apparently from an acute
Nimrod-inversion. It has been his practice to
go out in the evening shooting hares, with a
somewhat obsolete type of sporting rifle. He is
slightly myopic; his choice of a very bright
green suit for his sporting expeditions may,
perhaps, be an unconscious survival of the
protective colouring instinct. Latterly, he has
been obsessed by the hallucination (originating
in a dream) that a large hare has put on his own
spectacles, taken his own sporting rifle, and is
shooting at him. Sometimes, he says, the hare
misses him, but breaks a coffee cup which his
wife is holding in her hand at the door of their
house; the coffee falls on the nose of " the hare's
own child, the little hare," and burns it; the
little hare, holding a spoon in its paw, says,
" Oh, dear, such fun I do not understand." I
have had the case in hand for some time, but
have only just arrived at the truth about the
inhibition which has set up all the trouble. The
man is clearly a Chauvinist patriot, who has
suffered from some loss or shock during the war.
The word " hare " should have given me the
clue much earlier; it should really, of course,
be " Herr," a representative of the German

nation. He has been worried over the question of " Trading with the enemy," hence the " hare " uses *his own gun*, which is of an obsolete pattern, probably because he was equally worried over the munitions shortage. The " hare " misses him and hits his wife—an echo of the " German atrocities " scare; the loss of the coffee suggests the loss of trade due to the submarine warfare. Finally, the man was no doubt an enthusiast for the policy of " reprisals," and the fact that punishment recoils on " the Herr's own child, the little Herr," points to an intense subconscious desire for warfare upon undefended German towns. Possibly he wrote letters to the daily press, which were denied publication. What seems to clinch the identification of the " hare " with Germany is the fact that it wears spectacles; the young " Herr," too, is plainly deficient in the sense of humour.

Case VI.—Conrad ———, a pathetic instance of self-mutilation under strong subconscious suggestion. Originally it was an ordinary case of cannibalism, which had taken an autophagous direction. Conrad was a pronounced but not an irretrievable thumb-sucker. His mother, with the fatal tendency of well-meaning but uninstructed parents, adopted a deterrent policy. Nursery mythology, the juggernaut of the human species, had told her of a " great tall tailor " who always came to little boys who suck their thumbs. The bogey is represented, I need hardly say, as cutting off the thumbs with scissors. The myth in question is probably traceable to Mithras worship; but it may be obscurely derived from the classical conception of the Fates cutting the threads of the doomed person's life. The result might have been foreseen. Conrad is left alone; in an instant the supposedly succulent thumb finds its billet in his mouth. So far the action is merely instinctive, and could have led, at the worst, to nothing more serious than starvation-mania. But almost immediately " conscience," that fatal heritage of a fetishistic ancestry, gets to work; the intervention of the " great tall tailor " is momentarily expected, and under the urge of this impulse, the unhappy boy rushes to the work-basket, and performs on his own person an operation from which a qualified surgeon might have shrunk. The thumbs have gone, and this is, perhaps, not the worst part of the business: Conrad resolutely refuses to have new clothes made for him, although the orange pinafore he wears is no longer suitable to his time of life. When will parents learn?

Case VII.—Augustus ———, aged ten, was brought to me in an advanced stage of emaciation—the result of a starvation-complex, which had taken the not uncommon form of etnophobia. He had, I was told, been " plump, hearty, and healthy," and the fact that till lately he never found any difficulty about taking soup shows that there is (or was) no organic disability. It was a cold winter's day when the inhibition first manifested itself in the words " Take the nasty soup away, I won't have any soup to-day." The expression " to-day," had an obvious importance, the thermometer was somehow responsible for the inhibition ; probably the extreme heat of the soup was sensed as extreme cold   It is worth observing, however, that the father, a man of jocose habit, had often said to Augustus, " You'll find yourself in the soup, my boy, if you're not careful," or words to that effect, so that the trouble may have been, subconsciously, of longer standing. The treatment, in any case, was monstrously stupid—the parents refused to let him eat anything at all until he took soup. I have not

even dared to remonstrate with them as I should
like to, for fear of strengthening an Athamas-
complex in them which is already plainly
visible.   There is still some hope that the
symptoms are only those of gormandistic
perversion, and I have prescribed for the boy's
meals which begin with the dessert, and work
back gradually to the soup.   If the case fails
to respond to this treatment, we shall be forced
back on Bovril-injections, but I confess I recoil
from such methods.

Case VIII.—Philip ———, aged five, a victim
of seismic collapse.   The parents describe him
as incapable of sitting still at table ; an inveterate chair-tilter, he has been known to
clutch convulsively at the table-cloth as if in
search of support.   (There are no signs of loco-
motor ataxia, and the family physician has been
able to make nothing of the case.)   The original
source of the trouble is very hard to locate ;
he may have been born at sea ; or it may be a
suppression, e.g., was his mother or grandmother an artist's model?   (Mem.—Make
further enquiries.)   The tendency has certainly
been aggravated by the attitude of the parents,
who have been in the habit of saying, " Let us
see if Philip can be a little gentleman ; let me

see if he is able to sit still for once at table."
This combination of irony with an appeal to
class-consciousness has had the most devastating
effects. I have made a start by pointing out
that the habit of tying a napkin round the chin
must immediately be discontinued; subconsciously, the boy is no doubt gasping for breath
all through his meal-times.

Case IX.—John ———, aged eight, and
attending school regularly. The habit of carry-
ing the head in the air while walking is very
pronounced, but I have not yet dealt with the
case long enough to know whether this is due to
ordinary agorophobia, or to some more complicated condition, such as geophobia or sky-
fetishism. His statement that it is always his
rule to " look at the clouds that float by, and
see which of the swallows is cleverest at flying,"
may point to the last-named solution. He had,
recently, a collision with a dog, which resulted
in a tumble; this seems to have set up false
hydrophobia, for the other day, walking near
the river, he found himself unable to lower his
head, and a ducking was the consequence.
There was no life lost, because two passers-by,
with mistaken kindness, dragged him out with
their sticks. The right course would have been

to keep him in a vertical position throughout : the caradociac should never be allowed to assume the horizontal. The parents assure me that " Johnny never will forget what it is to be so wet," but I gravely fear that he will, and if he does, the effect on his subconsciousness does not bear thinking of. Already he is under the hallucination that the fishes are saying : " You have lost your writing-book," and unless great care is taken, it is to be feared that he will suffer from a permanent stoop.

Case X.—Robert ———, aged seven. The parents in this case were in great distress, because Robert insisted on going out in all weathers ; and there is a certain morbid love of rain which is unpleasantly suggestive of hypæthromania. But the boy is young, and it is doubtful whether we have to reckon on anything worse than claustrophobia at present. He seems to feel that his parents are unlawfully detaining him at home ; and his choice of a red umbrella probably indicates that he is in a state of revolt. I have told the parents that his wishes in the matter must on no account be thwarted : " Your son," I told them, " will be developing into a great aviator one of these days."

XI

A FORGOTTEN INTERLUDE

XI

A FORGOTTEN INTERLUDE

Bzz! Bang! Bzz! (*indistinct voice of an elderly don is heard in the middle of a lecture*) . . . weached itth perfection in Gway'th Elegy. The dithtinctive note, then, of eighthteenth thentuwy litewature ith that of technical perfection within a vewy limited wange of performanth. It wath time, perhapth, that the Fwench Wevolution came to dithturb the thecure domination of thothe conventional ideath which were thweatening the human geniuth with thtagnathion. Amid much that wath wegwettable in that movement, thith at leatht ith to be put down to itth cwedit, that it opened the way to a weadjuthtment of litewawy valueth and a higher thenthe of the poththibilitieth of human achievement. (*A prolonged cough, followed by silence.*)

(*The Operator*): London calling! That was Mr. William Donkinson, lecturing to you on Eighteenth Century Literature. Mr. William

Donkinson. We are now continuing the news bulletin since half-past six. The Test Match. The closing score when stumps were drawn in the Test Match was as follows: Australia 569 for seven wickets. The English team, it will be remembered, was all out for 173. Plucky waterman saves life at Chiswick. This morning, at a quarter past ten, shouts of help were heard from the Embankment close to Ponder's Row, Chiswick. James Bates, a waterman, whose attention was called to the cries by a bystander, jumped into the water, and rescued Susie, the five-year-old daughter of Mr. and Mrs. Holmes, of 17 Sunbury Place, Chiswick. The little one is believed to have fallen into the water accidentally while playing. The Unemployed Demonstration. The crowd in Trafalgar Square is now assuming threatening dimensions. Threatening dimensions are now being assumed by the crowd which has collected in Trafalgar Square to voice the grievances of the Unemployed. Mr. Popplebury, the Secretary of the National Movement for Abolishing Theatre Queues, has been urging the crowd to sack the National Gallery. The desirability of sacking the National Gallery is being urged by Mr. Popplebury, Secretary of the National Movement for Abolishing Theatre Queues. . . . One moment, please. . . . London calling; continuation of news bulletin from reports which have just come to hand. The crowd in Trafalgar Square is now proceeding, at the instigation of Mr. Popplebury, Secretary of the National Movement for Abolishing Theatre Queues, to sack the National Gallery. The National Gallery was first erected in 1838, to house the famous Angerstein collection of pictures, and has been considerably added to since. A new wing, designed by Mr. E. M. Barry, R.A., was added in 1876. It contains many well-known pictures by Raphael, Titian, Murillo, and other artists. It is now being sacked by the crowd, on the advice of Mr. Popplebury, Secretary of the National Movement for Abolishing Theatre Queues. That concludes the news bulletin for the moment; you will now be connected with the band at the Savoy Hotel. (*Dance music on the gramophone.*)

Hullo, everybody! London calling. You will now be given the weather report for to-morrow. The weather report for to-morrow now beginning. Fine generally, with occasional showers in the South and a continuous

downpour in the North.   The wind will be
violent in England, and in Scotland will probably assume the dimensions of a hurricane.
High tide at London Bridge 7.15.   That was
the weather report for to-morrow.   Continuation of the News Bulletin.   The Test Match.
The latest weather reports from Australia announce that a light rain is falling, and the
wicket will probably be somewhat sticky when
the Australians take the field to-morrow morning.   The Unemployed Demonstration.   The
crowd is now pouring through the Admiralty
Arch, and is advancing towards the back of
the Government Buildings in Whitehall in a
threatening manner.   The Admiralty Arch is
being poured through by a crowd, lately collected in Trafalgar Square, and the back of the
Government Buildings in Whitehall is being
approached in a threatening manner.   The
Admiralty Arch, designed by Sir Aston Webb,
was erected in 1910 as part of the national
memorial to Queen Victoria.   One moment,
please. . . .   The crowd has now collected in
the neighbourhood of the artificial water in
St. James' Park, and is throwing empty bottles
at the water-fowl.   Empty bottles are being
discharged by the crowds at the water-fowl on

the artificial water in St. James' Park. So far, no casualties have been reported. That concludes the News Bulletin for the moment.

Sir Theophilus Gooch, well-known for his many philanthropic schemes, will now address you on the Housing of the Poor. A lecture on the Housing of the Poor will now be delivered by Sir Theophilus Gooch, K.B.E. Sir Theophilus, it will be remembered, has for many years been chairman of the Committee for the Inspection of Insanitary Dwellings, and speaks with authority on his subject. Eh, what's that? One moment, please. . . . From reports which have just come to hand it appears that Sir Theophilus Gooch, who was on his way to this station, has been intercepted by the remnants of the crowd still collected in Trafalgar Square, and is being roasted alive. Born in 1879, Sir Theophilus Gooch entered the service of Messrs. Goodbody, the well-known firm of brokers. He very soon attracted the notice of his employers. However, nothing was proved, and Sir Theophilus retired with a considerable fortune. His retirement did not mean idleness; he has been prominent during the last ten years on many Committees connected with social improvement. He is now being roasted alive

by a crowd in Trafalgar Square. He will,
therefore, be unable to deliver his lecture to
you on the Housing of the Poor. You will be
connected instead with the Savoy Band for a
few minutes. (*Gramophone.*)

Hullo everybody! London calling. Continuation of News bulletin. Famous film
actress arrives at Southampton. Miss Joy
Gush, the well-known film actress, landed
this afternoon at Southampton. Interviewed
by the Press, Miss Gush said she had had a
capital crossing. Unemployed Demonstrations
in London. The crowd has now passed
along Whitehall, and at the suggestion of
Mr. Popplebury, Secretary of the National
Movement for Abolishing Theatre Queues, is
preparing to demolish the Houses of Parliament with trench mortars. The use of trench
mortars for demolishing the Houses of Parliament is being recommended by Mr. Popplebury, Secretary of the National Movement for
Abolishing Theatre Queues. The building of
the existing Houses of Parliament was begun in
1840. The designs were those of Sir Charles
Barry. The structure roughly forms a parallelo-
gram, 900 feet in length by 300 in width. The
internal decorations, frescoes, and statues are

deservedly admired. The building is made of magnesian limestone from Yorkshire, a material which is unfortunately liable to rapid decay. At present, in any case, it is being demolished with trench mortars under the influence of Mr. Popplebury, Secretary of the National Movement for Abolishing Theatre Queues. The three towers are 300 feet, 320 feet, and 346 feet high respectively. The Clock Tower, 320 feet in height, has just fallen to the ground, together with the famous clock, Big Ben, which used to strike the hours on a bell weighing nine tons. Greenwich time will not be given this evening by Big Ben, but will be given from Edinburgh on Uncle Leslie's repeating watch. Uncle Leslie's repeating watch will be used for giving Greenwich time this evening, instead of Big Ben, which has just fallen to the ground, under the influence of trench mortars. One moment, please. . . . Fresh reports, which have just come to hand, announce that the crowd have secured the person of Mr. Wotherspoon, the Minister of Traffic, who was attempting to make his escape in disguise. He has now been hanged from a lamp-post in the Vauxhall Bridge Road. One of the lamp-posts in the Vauxhall Bridge Road has been utilized by the

crowd for the purpose of hanging Mr. Wotherspoon, the Minister of Traffic. The crowd is
now returning along Whitehall. One moment,
please. . . . The British Broadcasting Company regrets that one item in the news has been
inaccurately given; the correction now follows.
It was stated in our news bulletin that the
Minister of Traffic had been hanged from a
lamp-post in the Vauxhall Bridge Road. Subsequent and more accurate reports show that
it was not a lamp-post but a tramway post
which was used for this purpose. A tramway
post, not a lamp-post, was used by the crowd
for the purpose of hanging the Minister of
Traffic. The next three items in our pro-
gramme are unavoidably cancelled; you will
now be connected up with the Savoy Band
again. (*More gramophone, which stops suddenly
with a loud report.*)

Hullo everybody! London calling. The
Savoy Hotel has now been blown up by the
crowd. That noise which you heard just now
was the Savoy Hotel being blown up by the
crowd, at the instigation of Mr. Popplebury,
Secretary of the National Movement for Abolishing Theatre Queues. One moment, please. . . .
The more unruly members of the crowd are

now approaching the British Broadcasting Company's London station with a threatening demeanour. A threatening demeanour is being exhibited by the crowd which is now approaching the B.B.C.'s London station. One moment, please. . . . Mr. Popplebury, Secretary of the National Movement for Abolishing Theatre Queues, with several other members of the crowd, is now in the waiting room. They are reading copies of the *Radio Times*. Good-night everybody ; good-night.